What Does It Mean To Be A Manager?

Five Phases of Employee Performance and Eighteen Tasks of Management

D1565992

Gil Herman

What Does It Mean To Be A Manager?

For information about this title, or to order other materials,
contact the author:
Gil Herman
Managing Horizons
Gil@ManagingHorizons.com
708-207-1879

What Does It Mean To Be A Manager?

PREFACE

I stand on the shoulders of many giants who laid the foundations on which we continue to build our understanding and practices of management – the art and science of getting important work done through direction and collaboration with others. There is little here that is brand new, although there are a number of twists to what is more established.

I have been a manager and trained new and experienced managers for 40-plus years. Many of us "missed that day in school" or have forgotten some of the best practices we picked up along the way. This book is intended to teach – or remind – us about our role and tasks of management in the context of employee performance.

I endeavored to make the learning more accessible by writing a business novel using a coaching dialogue with my daughter based on some of her real-world experiences. Most of the conversations were not face-to-face, so I introduced the idea that Ariel took some notes she kept in a binder. Ariel's Binder serves as the appendix to the book.

I wish to thank the many people who read this work in progress and provided candid input for its improvement, especially some of my Vistage members, coaching clients, and friends, particularly Rob Bellmar and Blaine Rada. I also thank my daughter Meridian Herman Lupu for her book design and graphics expertise without which this volume would be just words. And I express my deep love and gratitude to Ariel for her encouragement to write this book as a way to document this part of my life's journey, to help her and others learn from my experiences, and to ensure we are each appropriately represented in our dialogue and actions in the book.

And finally – I dedicate this to all managers in all walks of life. May it serve in some way to help you live a life of significance – because what you do really matters.

Gil Herman
Gil@ManagingHorizons.com
November, 2014

TABLE OF CONTENTS

What Does It Mean To Be A Manager?

Chapter 1: EMPLOYEE PERFORMANCE PHASES

"Hey Dad, in my new job, I'll have five people formally reporting to me, and I'll be inside a more-structured organization than I've worked in before. I'm concerned I may not yet have the skills to be as successful as I want to be in these circumstances. I'm wondering what will be different. What does it mean to be a manager?"

This from my daughter, Ariel, recently turned 25. After college she had been a paid volunteer for a year serving a rural community with real needs and living her values of continuous learning and giving back. They liked her work and skills along with her sincere desire to continue to learn and serve. As the volunteer year was ending, they asked her to stay on as a full time and full salaried employee. She and her manager had always had such open and mutually supportive communication, that it was almost a no-brainer to stay and continue her work.

She put grad school on the back burner and further dedicated herself to the important work she was doing. She gave a commitment for at least one more year and continued learning. She grew into additional responsibilities, including a bit of coaching and training of her state-wide counterparts as well as doing some informal supervision of local staff.

After a total of three years – and a deeply evolving personal relationship with a man who had relocated to the big city, she made the very difficult decision to leave the rural position and move to the city with him. That meant finding a new job – her first real search – at a very tight time in the economy. She had found a small number of opportunities in her chosen field – her passion – but nothing was perfect. One would be a long commute. Another would require being on-call several evenings and weekends. Still another opportunity was potentially emerging to continue to work at least part-time with her former employer from a distance while a new, local position was being designed.

Employee Performance Phases

The position she accepted was slightly different work in a closely related field. It would be a short commute, much less on-call time, with a potential to grow it into something bigger over time. Her direct supervisor with whom she had interviewed, seemed like a nice guy and supportive of her coming on board. He felt she could add value to the organization given her prior work experience and expressed values. They both acknowledged her lack of formal management experience and felt those skills would naturally develop with experience.

So, after moving to the far away city, she was home for a brief visit before starting her new job. After she shared some of the overall mission of the organization and some of her goals, she wanted to talk more about her future role.

"I understand my goals and am looking forward to doing the work. However, I will officially be managing people and I haven't really done that before. I'm not sure I'll get the training and support I need to be successful in this role now that I've taken it."

"Well Ariel, as you know, I have been in management for over 40 years and have trained and coached managers and leaders of organizations from small companies through Fortune 500. I have some ideas I could share with you.

What Does It Mean To Be A Manager?

However, you are first and foremost my daughter, and we have a special loving relationship. I wouldn't want to do or say anything that might change that to a professional relationship."

"Dad, I think we can do both and make it work. Maybe just wait until I ask you a question or seek your advice. Now, I'm asking you – what is the role of a manager? I mean, what am I supposed to do?"

"OK. It's a deal. First, how would you answer your own question – what is the role of a manager?"

Ariel didn't have to think long. "A manager is supposed to help his or her direct reports – I don't like the word 'subordinates' – to do the job they were hired for. That, in turn, will help the organization serve its clients and achieve its mission."

"So, let me see if I am hearing you correctly," I responded. "The overall role of the manager is to help the organization achieve its goals and to do that through the work results of his or her direct reports. Have I got that right?"

"Sounds like you heard me correctly. Was my answer right?" As a student, Ariel was always one who was willing to volunteer an answer, and she also wanted to know if she got the right answer.

"It's a fine answer – for now," I replied. "Let's see if and how it might change as you gain experience and think about what you're doing." I continued – "Let's start with your experience and understanding of what employees do. Let's not worry about any particular employee or any particular position in any organization. Consider your own experience and that of others you know or have observed. Tell me about the life of an employee in any given role."

"Well, she – I'll use 'she' because I can relate to that much better from my own experience - she starts the job on day 1 and is eager to do it well – and get compensated fairly for what she does. She's excited about all the new people she'll work with and the opportunity to increase her knowledge and skills. After a while – and that could be days, weeks or months depending on the complexity of the job – she should be performing at the required level. Then she just keeps on doing that. She keeps doing the job and performing well."

"Great description! As we're sitting together, let's create a diagram of this as we go along. You're describing how a person performs over time," I said as I drew a vertical line labeled 'Performance' and a horizontal line labeled 'Time' with an arrow pointing to the future. This is what we have so far."

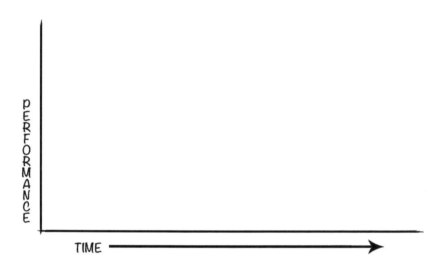

I added, "Before we can go further, would we have to know what a person will be responsible for in this job?"

"Of course," said Ariel. "There should be some idea of why the job is needed and what goals the employee has to achieve. It would be good to know what knowledge and skills someone would need and the specific requirements of the job," she suggested.

"OK. You've just described what I consider the first phase of the performance cycle. I call it 'Framing' and most of it happens before any given employee even starts the job. Further, what you called 'the specific requirements of the job' I refer to as the 'Target Performance Level'."

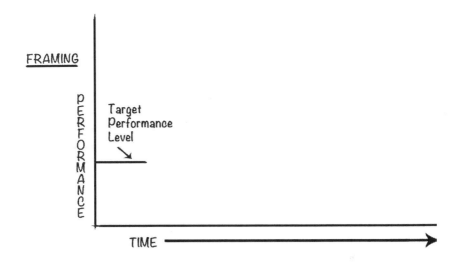

"OK," Ariel nodded. "And we also have to find someone to do the job."

"Absolutely," I concurred. "Now, assuming you've made a hire, does every employee start out at the same level of performance on day one?" I asked.

"No," she replied. "Each individual comes with her unique

set of knowledge and skills. Some may be fairly close to what you called the Target Performance Level; some will need more training to get up to speed." She took the pen and marked a couple X's to show different starting points. "And they each may have different learning curves to get up to the required level," she said adding a curved line connecting each X to the Target Performance Level.

"Excellent! Let's call that phase 'Training'. How long it takes depends on the starting point, the complexity of the job, and a number of other factors we'll come back to." I took the pen and labeled the second phase accordingly.

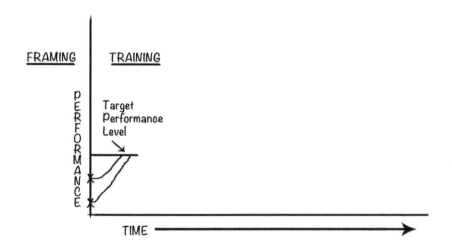

Employee Performance Phases

"Once someone has achieved the target performance level for her job, what usually happens next?"

"Well," responded Ariel, "I know that once I learned my last job, my manager started giving me a bit more work to do. She explained to me that I had learned the job well and that my workload would increase over time in that same role. She'd keep giving me more and more until I couldn't handle anything further, then try to keep me at that level."

"So the amount of work required increases over time along with expectations of continuing to perform well with the increased load," I said extending the Target Performance Level with an upward slope.

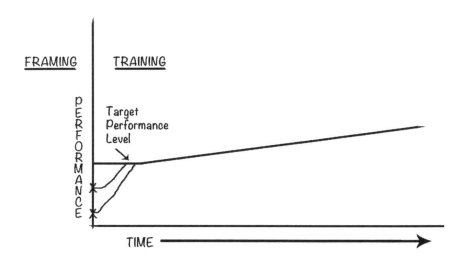

What Does It Mean To Be A Manager?

"It sure seemed that way over the three years. But I liked the continuing challenges, variety, and additional responsibilities."

"And were you always performing with the same level of results?"

"Most of the time, sure. And there were times I was doing even better," she replied, "as well as – only a few times – I was not keeping up with the requirements."

"That's very normal. Let's call the third phase 'Sustaining'. The aim is to continually and consistently perform at the Target Performance Level. And, "I said adding the label and a squiggly line, "our generic employee will likely keep doing the same role with increasing requirements over time and will typically perform at, somewhat above, or somewhat below those increasing requirements."

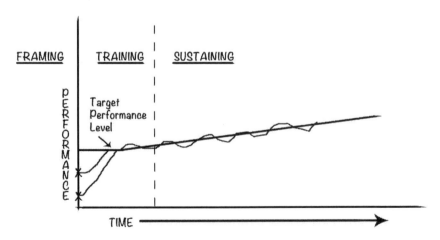

Employee Performance Phases

I continued, "Ariel, from what you've seen, does this Sustaining phase ever stop or change?"

"I know people – good employees – who have stayed in the same role for years sustaining their performance of increasing requirements. In fact, I know some people – older like you, Dad – who kept at a specific job until they retired."

"Ouch! Nice jab at your old man! Do you know others who moved beyond sustaining at some point?"

"Of course. I guess I was one of them. My manager and I talked about how I'd been able to meet the ever-increasing requirements in my role and that it was time to take on some additional special projects with more responsibility. I loved that. I learned even more. I got to work with more people, especially outside the office. I was just starting to get a little restless, feeling that I had mastered my job. These new responsibilities reignited my fire."

"I see. Some people – like you – do consistently well over time sustaining their performance above the required level." I drew the squiggly line above the Target Performance Level. "Then an opportunity that is valuable to the organization is presented as a bit of a stretch. Our generic employee is now in the 'Gaining' phase. As you described it, there is more challenge and variety in the job; more opportunities for learning and contributing a greater impact on the organization's goals. If appropriate, this could eventually lead to a promotion – a new role for her in the organization. Of course, if and when that happens, the employee starts the cycle over again with Training, then Sustaining." I added to the diagram to indicate the Gaining phase.

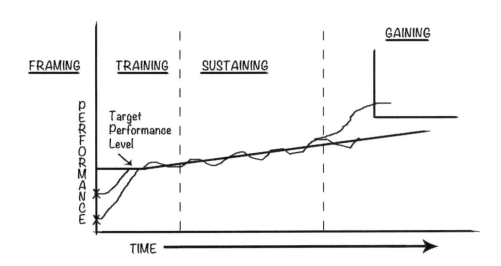

Employee Performance Phases

"I get it!" Ariel replied enthusiastically. "When I was invited to stay on as a full time paid employee, I moved into an expanded role and had new things to learn and do in addition to most of my former tasks. Later I got a title change and still more responsibilities, including some supervisory work. I guess I may have gone through Training, Sustaining, and Gaining a few times."

"I believe you did," I acknowledged. "Now, one further observation. Did you ever notice anyone who in the Sustaining phase seemed to be missing her requirements, perhaps more and more often? What happened then?"

"I wasn't always aware of other people's performance, but there were signs of trouble. I can think of a few co-workers who may have had various performance issues. One of them seemed to have just given up. He shared with me that he was feeling burned out and didn't feel like he wanted to do the job any more. My manager – who was also his manager – had a talk with him and he seemed to reengage. I'd say he went back to sustaining his performance, but I don't know the details."

"This is the phase I call 'Draining'. It happens when someone has been sustaining for some time, but for some reason the performance drops off. Typically it is due to a

What Does It Mean To Be A Manager?

decrease in ability and/or desire to do the job." I added a label and squiggly line moving downward. "At some point, it's important to determine if the draining is due to a decrease in ability and/or a decrease in desire," I said adding the question mark and labels on the diagram.

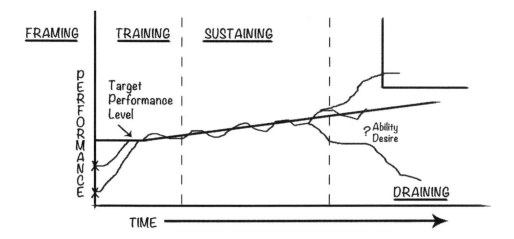

I continued, "This can be due to burn out like with your colleague, or other internal and external factors. It sounds like your manager was able to help him re-engage. That's one thing that can happen. What else …?"

Ariel jumped in before I could even finish the question. "A friend of mine from college told me about his experience. He was getting bored with the job and his performance was dropping off. They put him on what they called a 'Performance Improvement Plan'. After about a month, he was back on track, but told his manager he was really getting tired of the job he was doing. My friend told me that his manager said the organization saw potential in him and that now that he was showing he could do the job – the ability was there, but not the desire – they were going to look for another position in the organization to move him into. He was given a lateral move to a different role and, so far, is very happy and doing well. I guess he probably had to go through Training and Sustaining in that new role, too."

"Right! Not all organizations would consider moving someone to another role – or even have another role that would be appropriate and available."

Ariel added, "I guess then, that if the employee doesn't get back on track or there isn't another place for him, then - as I've heard you say – 'he is made available to industry'."

"By George, I think you've got it!" I exclaimed in perfect imitation of Henry Higgins from My Fair Lady. "So, going back to your original comment regarding the role of a manager - A manager is supposed to help his or her direct reports to do the job they were hired for. Now that we know the Phases of Employee Performance, a more specific if overly simplistic clarification is that the manager's job is to identify which phase each employee is in and help her be successful in that phase and prepare her for whatever might be next. Let's take a break and come back to more specifics on some Tasks of Management corresponding to each Phase."

Ariel, to show her understanding and sense of humor said, "I'll make us some lunch. I've been through training and have mastered the skills of making a toasted cheese sandwich. I believe I am well above the target performance level, so I'll add to the requirements some spicy tomato soup and pickles. Perhaps I can get a promotion to master chef."

FORMULATE and ARTICULATE

Chapter 2: FORMULATE and ARTICULATE

After the delicious lunch and some collaborative clean up, we went back to our drawing and discussion.

"So, Dad," suggested Ariel, "I was thinking that before someone even gets started in her job, the organization has to know that they have a job that needs to be done."

"Right you are! This includes one of the first – what I call – 'Tasks of Management'. Before a manager hires someone, he – or she – (let's use "he" to avoid confusion with the "she" we used for the employee) - must be clear on the

What Does It Mean To Be A Manager?

organization's vision, mission, values, and how those translate into strategies, goals, and objectives for his part of the organization. So the first – and continuing- task of management is to Formulate the division or department goals."

"Sounds like a manager needs to know what he's trying to accomplish before he sets out to do it or have someone else do it," Ariel replied.

"That's right – but it's certainly not always the way all managers approach things. I can't count the number of times I've worked with managers who get caught up in what some have called an 'activity trap'. Sometimes a manager just keeps doing whatever he's been doing without first making sure it's the right thing to do. It's important to step back every once in a while and make sure the path you're on will lead to the destination you desire."

"Well how should a manager set his goals so he can avoid the activity trap?" Ariel inquired.

"The first thing he should do is read and have conversations with his management and peers to be sure he understands the organization's vision, mission, values and strategies. Different organizations have some or all of the above, although it can be confusing because many organizations use the same words to describe different things. 'Vision' and 'mission' are often reversed. And ..."

"Whoa! Wait a minute!" interrupted Ariel. "Different organizations may use the same word to mean different things? That's just crazy!"

"It happens all the time and does lead to some confusion, especially for a new hire who may have come from another organization with a different understanding. What I've found is that the word or words used is much less important than ensuring that everyone acts in accordance with the concepts."

"What do you mean?"

"I've facilitated dozens of strategic planning retreats with numerous organizations over the years. If we were not careful, the conversations would convert to a wordsmithing exercise where the focus was on choosing the exact words, rather than ensuring that everyone was aligned with the meaning – especially the Why We Exist. It's a fine line, because there should be something in writing that captures the essence of the organization. For example, all organizations have customers – other organizations or individuals who use the products or services provided. It's important to talk about who are these customers and why they need what they need and how they need it to be provided. It's less valuable – in my opinion – to go back and forth about whether to call them clients, customers, stakeholders, users, or such like when in the midst of a planning process. That distinction can be done later if it is really needed."

"OK – off the soap box. What I want to know for now is how all that effects my job as a manager?" Ariel sure knows how to stop my pontificating at times.

"Thanks for bringing me back. We'll save the discussion about vision, mission, values, and organization culture for another time. So for now, let's assume the manager – 'he' - has some understanding of all that stuff and is personally aligned with and committed to it. We'll also assume the organization has done and is following a strategic plan that sets some goals for the next 1 to at least 3 years. What's your guess as to what the manager's next task is given that scenario?"

"Well, I guess he would need to come up with some goals for his own department," Ariel tentatively suggested.

FORMULATE and ARTICULATE

"Exactly! He needs to take his understanding of the organization's goals laid out in the strategic plan and formulate goals for his own department that help to achieve the organization's goals. These may start out as only qualitative – only setting a general direction for things that need to be achieved."

"That sounds pretty high-level, Dad" interjected Ariel. "From my experience, I know they have to be much more detailed because I'm going to have a review to discuss how I performed against some pretty specific targets."

"Right again, Ariel. Once the manager has determined the general direction, he needs to add more detail to make what's called a 'SMART' goal – Specific, Measurable, Achievable, Relevant, and Time-bound. In their best presentation, they should paint a picture of what conditions should be observable at a pre-determined future date. It should also be clear how creating that condition will contribute to the organization's overall goals."

"That sounds easier said than done," responded Ariel.

"Setting SMART goals is one of the most important tasks of management. When done well, those SMART goals serve as the foundations of success for the manager, all his employees, and the organization. But, you're right, it's also one of the more difficult tasks and needs to be done with considerable diligence."

Ariel commented, "Well even if he does a great job formulating SMART goals, it sounds like it may have been done in a vacuum. How does he assure they are the right goals to achieve? And, how does he make sure he has the right people and resources to achieve them?"

"I call that task of management 'Articulate'. He has to talk to others – bosses, peers, current direct reports, possibly other departments, customers, suppliers, and so on to share what he plans for his department to achieve and be sure everyone's on the same page. Part of that discussion is to also articulate the staffing and other resources needed."

"And what happened to our employee? Where does she come into these the formulation and articulation of these SMART goals?" questioned Ariel.

"Well, if she is a current employee, she may have had a say in helping formulate or articulate the goals. For example, based on her understanding of the qualitative goal – the direction – she may have been asked to formulate her personal goals that would feed up to the manager. If she is new to her position, these goals may have been set before she was hired or promoted."

"So, what's important here, I think," suggested Ariel, "is that before a person even starts the job – or a new performance cycle - the manager has to already have the SMART goals nailed down."

"That would be ideal," I replied. "However, some situations change and goals may get re-prioritized, added or dropped. It's important to keep goals up to date to ensure everyone is working on the right stuff. We'll come back to that later. For now, just as you said, the manager should have formulated and articulated the goals up front."

"OK – hold it right there. I need a glass of iced tea before we talk about some other stuff. Would you like something to drink, too?"

"Water would be fine for me. I'd like exactly 8 ounces in a tumbler, no ice, and placed on this table in 3 minutes. How's that for SMART?"

"There's a word that would follow "smart" I could use to respond. I'll just say, 'I know exactly what to do'."

Chapter 3: DESIGNATE

Several weeks later after Ariel had returned to her out-of-state job, she called to say they were starting a new project. She had created SMART goals for the project and it was clear she needed to fill a new staff position. That person would be the key contributor to the new project, but would also work on several on-going department goals.

"My boss said there's an internal candidate he'd like me to consider. I think that person is OK, but not quite the right fit. There's a different internal candidate that I believe might be a better fit with the rest of the team, but she's not as

---

knowledgeable.   Or, I could go outside to try to find someone."

"Who will make the decision – you or your boss?" I asked, knowing that how we proceeded would be somewhat determined by her answer.

"He assured me it's my decision and he will support it whatever way I choose to go. Of course, he also let me know that I will have to deal with the consequences of my decision, including how to tell one or both of the internal candidates that they were not selected."

"Well that's good. That seems to indicate that he feels you are ready for that level of responsibility and accountability."

"I guess so - but I'm still not sure how to make the best decision. Any ideas how I should think this through?"

"Ariel, you're ready to learn more about the next task of management. I call it 'Designate'. This is where you source, interview and select a person for a position that needs to be filled. I say 'a position that needs to be filled' rather than 'a job that needs to get done' because you said you're looking for someone to work on a specific project *and* that they'll have other work to do as well, perhaps continuing beyond the time scope of the project. Right?"

"Absolutely. We're working with limited financial resources and need to leverage this person as much as we can."

"OK. Let's go through some of the steps you'll need to take in order so you can get a good fit for the position. What do you think you need to do first?"

"Put the word out – tell people I know that we're looking for someone.   Put ads on the internet and maybe in the newspaper," she quickly suggested.

"Well, what would you tell people or put in an ad?"

"We have to tell them the organization, the title and position description, who to contact if interested. Should we specify the salary range and benefits?"

"Whoa there! That's a lot of information. How much you say will vary by market and kinds of people you want to attract. Before you get there, let me ask you – have you created a written position description?"

"I have the written department SMART goals and the same for the project." Ariel clarified.

"That's great! Based on the results you need this person to achieve, do you have a list of the knowledge and skills they need to use?"

"We have some. They need to be an expert in the field. They need to have at least 5 years experience working with clients and using our community resources. They need to be fully proficient in Microsoft Office and how to use the internet to conduct searches related to precedents. And a few more like that. Is that what you mean?"

"Well, I don't know the field or position description, so I'll stay general. One mistake hiring managers often make is to list lots of skills and knowledge they think is necessary to do the job. Those managers are looking for 'Superman' – or woman – who may be very difficult to find. I believe it helps to make the list, then prioritize the importance and urgency of each skill and area of knowledge. One way to do this is to ask yourself, 'What is absolutely critical for someone to know and be able to do on day one? What skills and knowledge do they have to be able to use by 3 months, 6 months, one year?'"

"So, you're saying I may not need someone who is an expert in the field right away because we can train them on that knowledge? And, I may not need someone who's already well networked in our community, because we can introduce them around?"

"Possibly. As you start sourcing, it's important that you have a base line for what are 'must have' versus 'nice to have'."

"That makes sense. I believe I can do that with some input from my boss and HR."

"Another thing to consider might be what used to be called 'attitude'. I prefer to think of it as 'culture fit'. If your organization has a set of values and norms that it expects from employees, you might include those in your position description."

"Are you saying I need to put all this information in an ad!? Dad – think Twitter! 140 characters max!" Ariel exclaimed incredulously.

"Hey - calm down. What I'm suggesting is you create this full description along with the SMART goals to help you prepare an interview guide and an assessment process. A help-wanted ad should serve two purposes – attract potential candidates and help interested people understand whether they have the qualifications to apply for the position."

"So, keep it brief, inviting, and specify must-have minimums?"

"That's right. Your HR department or an outside recruiter can help you wordsmith, if necessary."

"What about compensation? Remember, I asked whether the ad should include salary and benefits."

"What have you seen during your personal searches or from 'comparison shopping'?"

"Some ads say nothing and I'm left to wonder. Some say commensurate with experience. Some list a range. Some say 'competitive salary'. It's all so ambiguous," she sighed. "Indicating a range may help people consider whether they want to apply. I knew if the salary mentioned was too low compared to what I was looking for, I was either over-qualified for what they were seeking or would have a lot of negotiating to do. If it was much higher than what I'd been making, although enticing, I'd wonder if I had enough experience to fill the role. I guess the default I saw most often were 'competitive salary' or 'commensurate with experience'. Then I had to decide whether to apply based more on the work than the compensation."

What Does It Mean To Be A Manager?

"So, depending on the position, geography, local economic conditions, and so on, the listing of compensation may or may not be helpful in attracting the right people. Is that what you're concluding?"

"I'm still not sure. I guess this is another item to discuss with HR. We may have some specific guidelines I'm not aware of. Or – maybe even some samples to build from."

"OK – for now, let's move on to other aspects of Designate. We'll assume you've figured out how to source and now have a candidate pool – internal and/or external – who have passed through some initial screening and are all potentially the person you're looking for. What's next?"

"That's easy! I have to interview them and select the best one to hire."

"Easier said than done. Here are a few questions to consider for the interview process. How many times and in what ways will each candidate be interviewed? Who will do the interviewing? What questions will they ask? What information about the organization and the position will be shared, by whom and when? Will there be any assessments or tests to validate abilities? How will you compare candidates? And many more."

"Well Dad, based on my experience and what I've seen here and at other places I worked – even when I applied to college – the answers to those questions is, 'it depends'."

"On what does it depend?" I asked, not wanting to let her off the hook.

"I think it depends on how important the position is and for how long you're looking for someone to fill that position or work with the organization.   The more significant the decision, the more the process seems to involve things like assessments, multiple interviewers, and lots of questions."

"So, for this position you've been telling me you're seeking to fill – what process do you think will give you a necessary, relevant, and sufficient way to evaluate each candidate?" Like most hiring managers, I believed Ariel had a pretty good sense of what to do, but wanted her to articulate it against the criteria I suggested – necessary, relevant and sufficient. Whatever process she would use would have to focus on a candidate's experience and values-oriented behaviors. She'd have to be careful asking hypothetical questions that might indicate good thinking and interviewing skills, but not be as reliable to determine actual behaviors that have been demonstrated previously and would be likely to continue. And then there's the challenge of not asking enough

What Does It Mean To Be A Manager?

questions to get the information you need to compare candidates – or asking too many questions that don't add anything further.

"So, this is a position – especially the project – that will require someone with some knowledge and experience in the field. He or she will work with lots of different people inside and outside the organization. And the person will have to be good with the computer – at least Word and Excel to record data and generate reports. We'll need to make sure they talk with HR, me, my boss, a couple of potential co-workers, and maybe a couple people from other community organizations that they'll need to collaborate with."

"What else?" I asked, sensing she was on a roll.

"Let's see. That person will be out in the community a lot, so I guess having a chance to talk to the candidates in various venues to see what they notice and how they interact would be useful. And, in addition to seeing samples of relevant reports they've created in other positions, we should give them some background on a real case study and have them generate a report and make recommendations for next steps. If they can do that, they're really on their way to thinking and acting like the person I need!" She was clearly getting excited about the possibilities.

"Great! Those are terrific ideas on how to get some sense of the person's abilities and behaviors. What are some questions you or others should ask? Remember, you want to assess the degree to which you think the person can do the job and fit the culture - *and* you will need some way to compare candidates to one another. "

"Dad, you might not understand the position in enough detail to help me with specific questions. But, does this make sense? I need to look at the 'must have' knowledge and skills as well as the values, and have at least one open-ended question for each of those," she proposed.

"Exactly! If you have a set of questions around what's most important, and a way of assessing how each candidate responded, you'll be well on your way to comparing all the candidates against the same criteria."

"And," she said, "we can figure out who will ask which questions so we get corroboration without overdoing redundancy. As you said – 'necessary, relevant, and sufficient'."

"My experience of you, Ariel, is that you are great at sticking mostly to the facts without undue bias based on whether you like someone. How will you and the other interviewers 'score' how each candidate responded without that natural bias?"

"I'm thinking of creating a form for the interview report and how each candidate responded to each question. Those will be the 'facts'. I'll also put in a space for any additional comments such as 'I liked the person', 'She had appropriate eye contact' or 'He was constantly fidgeting with his pen'."

"OK. Here's an idea to help. Make a written list of the specific questions that will be asked and who will ask them. Provide space for the interviewer to briefly record the response – either during or after the interview. Then ask the interviewer – definitely *after* the interview - to assign a rating on a scale of 1 – 5, 5 being highest, for how well the response given suggests the candidate's likely ability to do that part of the job."

"So, if I'm the interviewer and I ask a specific question related to a must-have skill, I can jot down what the person said and score it on how well I think they'll be able to use that skill in this position. Sounds good. And if all the interviewers do the same thing for the questions they ask, we should be able to do a somewhat objective candidate comparison. Right?"

"Absolutely. Now, as to the comparison. A simple concise way I've done that is to create a spreadsheet listing vertically the skills, knowledge and values in column A. Next to each, I assign a weight on a scale of importance from 1 - 5, 5 being the highest. In this column, I might give a must-have skill a 5 if it's critical to have day 1. I might give a must-have skill a 4 if it needs to be developed by, say, 3 months. If I listed any nice-to-have items in column A, they would also have a weighting, but nothing higher than a 3."

Ariel said, "Hold on a moment. I want to draw a picture of this as we talk. I've already started a binder of notes and drawings. I'm sure there will be a few more things to add over time."

"Sounds like a great idea. Most of my clients do the same thing while we're working face-to-face and I can be sure we're accurate in our communication. If you want, feel free to send me a copy of your diagrams and I'll check them over."

 "Great. I'll do that. I've got this one started. What's next?"

"The next columns are headings for each candidate – two

columns each. In the first column is the rating of how the interviewer or interviewers scored the person's likely ability to apply the knowledge, skills or values to the position. The second column per candidate is the product of multiplying the weight by the rate per item in column A. I like this process for making it clearer where the strengths and differences are per candidate. "

Ariel jumped in - "And at the bottom of each candidate's second column, I could total up that candidate's overall score. Got it! Then I'll have a somewhat objective comparison along with the non-factual observations that each interviewer would have made."

Comparing Candidates		Candidate A		Candidate B		Candidate C		Candidate D	
Position:									
Skills, Knowledge and Values	Weight (1)	Average rate (2)	weight x rate	Average rate (2)	weight x rate	Average rate (2)	weight x rate	Average rate (2)	weight x rate
Skill 1									
Skill 2									
Skill 3									
...									
Knowledge 1									
Knowledge 2									
Knowledge 3									
...									
Value 1									
Value 2									
Value 3									
...									
Total									

(1) Weight - must have day 1 = 5, must have in 3 months = 4, nice to have 3, 2, or 1

(2) Average from all interviewers

"Sounds like you've got it!" I exclaimed.

"At that point, I can rank the candidates in descending order and determine which ones, if any, I want to move forward with. And I know HR and I will need to do reference checking to validate candidates' claims."

"Yes, and increasingly, organizations are doing internet searches to see how candidates have shown up online. Further, depending on the position, especially if the person will be handling any money or sensitive information, organizations may do a criminal background check and credit report. Be aware, that in most cases, the candidate is informed and must give permission for those checks to happen. And all candidates that make it through the previous steps must be treated equally with respect to what and how you check such information. Otherwise you open yourself and your organization up to discrimination claims of unfair hiring practices."

"Speaking of which, I know from an article I read, that there are some questions that we shouldn't ask. I believe it was things like 'What languages do you speak? Do you have a car? Do you have children?' The article said some of that kind of information can lead someone to assumptions about a person's background that have nothing to do with whether they can do the job."

"Right you are – to a point. For example, *if* the job requires that the employee needs to be fluent in a second language, then it's ok to ask *every* candidate. *If* the job requires them to use a non-company-provided vehicle to perform their job, then it's OK to ask *every* candidate for proof of a valid driver's license and their access to a vehicle. If the question is not relevant to the must-have aspects of the job, then it's probably best to steer away from them."

"That article said that sometimes information is entered on the job application, cover letter or resume, or the candidate makes reference to something without being asked. Is that OK?"

"You may not be able to stop someone from telling you things that could lead to a bias. But you and your fellow interviewers should do your best not to consider such things when making the hiring decision. Check with HR to see what laws and guidelines are currently in place."

"Oh – and one other thing I've experienced" added Ariel, "is some kind of psychological assessment. I think I had both an intelligence test and a personality assessment. What about those kinds of things?"

"That's an interesting question. Some companies for some positions want to get a sense of a candidate's thinking and behavioral preferences or styles. Such assessments can provide tremendous useful insight for how to manage and develop someone if and when hired. Two cautions: first, they have to be administered to every candidate who makes it to a predefined phase in your interviewing process. Otherwise, you set yourself up for possible discriminatory practices. Second, although some professionals I know swear by them, I believe they are not always an accurate way of predetermining how someone will act in a given set of conditions. They can provide good guidelines after a person is on board, but I'd be careful about depending on them to designate who to hire."

"Dad, this is all great stuff and I can put it to use immediately. One last thing we started to discuss earlier. What if I have one or more internal candidates that apply for the position – especially if I don't think they are the best candidate?"

"Now that we've discussed all this, how would you answer your own question?"

"Well, I guess I'd do all the same stuff as I'd do with the outside candidates. Ask the questions related to each of the must-have knowledge, skills, and values; review what they

---

say – or I know – about how they interact in the organization and with clients and suppliers. I guess I'd already know some of the answers based on my own observations, but it couldn't hurt to ask the same questions and give the ratings for comparison. Clearly, it's possible the internal candidate will show up with the highest total score. But, if not, then what?"

"I've looked at the total score for the *objective* comparison. However, there are pluses and minuses to consider *subjectively* as well. For example, some pluses might include that the person already knows the organization and culture, has positive relationships established, and this position represents an appropriate opportunity on their career path. Some minuses might be that the person is not a good fit with the culture of the department, that there is not a good backfill for the position being vacated, or it's viewed as a political maneuver rather than a good fit."

"It would seem that if we go through the fact-gathering, those subjective considerations might become less important," Ariel suggested.

"That's right. And that's how you would handle talking with the internal candidate who doesn't get the job. After you thank them for their interest and application, you can be specific about what must-have skills or knowledge were missing or lower ranked, and suggest ways those things could be developed for future opportunities. Do this with care and compassion, and it usually works out. There may still be disappointment, but hopefully as they get to know the person you do hire and see that person's performance, the internal candidate will agree that you made the right choice for the organization."

"When do I have that conversation? I assume not until after a different person has been offered and has accepted the job."

"That's how I'd do it typically. But if I'm clear earlier that the internal candidate will not be a good fit, I tell them so as soon as possible rather than leaving them hanging. Be careful not to hold on to the idea that if no one else shows up, you can settle for the internal candidate who's not a good fit. It usually doesn't work out in the long run."

"And when and how do we make an offer and negotiate with the preferred candidate?"

"My major recommendation is to hold off on any offers until you have interviewed all the candidates in the pool who passed through the initial screenings. Sometimes we can feel that we really like someone and believe they can do the job. Or someone says they have another offer pending and is pushing you to rush your decision. Wait so you can do the comparison to select your best options. Having said that, every situation is different. I suggest you work with HR on the policies and procedures they use."

"And salary negotiations?"

"Again, I suggest you work with HR. However, you should at least know what the organization has budgeted for the position and if and where you have any room to negotiate. In some cases, it is what it is. In other cases, you may have lots of leeway for the right person."

"OK – I'm ready to write up the questions related to the must haves, assign the interviewers and be sure they all know which questions to ask and how to score the answers. We already have a couple inside people who have expressed interest, and I'll work with HR to put the word out for others. And, I'll talk with my boss to clarify the budget and amount of leeway I have for negotiating."

"Great. Good luck. Let me know how it goes."

"OK. Love you. Bye."

INITIATE

Chapter 4: INITIATE

"Hey Dad! I hired Sue, an eager and experienced outside candidate," Ariel exclaimed when she called me a week and a half later. "She's got what it takes to really help us provide our services to the community. She's got experience in the field and has worked with people similar to our clients. She's also volunteered at non-profit organizations that provide services in our community."

"That sounds great, Ariel," I replied. "How'd it go telling the internal candidates?"

What Does It Mean To Be A Manager?

"I ended up with only two who expressed interest. One withdrew during the process, acknowledging that she didn't yet have the experience to do the job. The other was a bit disappointed, but is excited about what Sue can bring to our organization."

"Good work, Ariel. Keep an eye on each of them for further development. Maybe another opportunity will come about that could work for everyone."

"Of course," Ariel replied. Then, "Dad, I think I've got a pretty good sense of the tasks of a manager from formulating and articulating the goals and what to do to select and designate a new employee in a particular position. I feel I did good work on those tasks and now have Sue scheduled to start in two weeks. I'm really excited and energized to add her to the staff. I want to be sure she hits the ground running. What are some of the things I should be doing to help her get off to a good start?"

"You are now ready for the management task I call 'Initiate'. What are your ideas about what you need to do and how to get Sue started?" I prompted. "You might consider what worked or didn't work well for you when you started something new."

INITIATE

"What worked best for me was meeting with my supervisor on day 1 to go over the job again. I know when I interviewed, it was important to me to understand what the position was and to consider whether it was the right work and place for me. But to be honest, I also needed a job and was concerned with making a good impression. It was good to have the stress of the interview behind me so I could really dig into what my supervisor was telling me the job would really entail."

"Ok, what else?" I knew she could draw more on her own experiences and wanted her to feel the confidence that comes from having lived through some of this herself.

"If I go further back, I remember when I went off to college. The first thing they did was put us with other people so we could experience some of the orientation activities together and begin to immediately make some friends and build community. We also had an upperclassman assigned to show us around and answer any questions we had. That was really helpful."

I could tell she was remembering fondly the beginnings of her independence from home and family and was excited about the care she was experiencing on that new phase of her life journey. "What else do you remember from your college orientation?" I asked to help her probe deeper into her memories.

"I remember when you and Mom drove me to campus to help me get settled in. The biggest question was where was my dorm room and what would my roommate be like. As you know, I enjoy reading a map and finding my own way, but it was great that they had volunteer guides all over the place. And then, when I found my room, I was so thrilled to meet my roommate – and her family. Everybody joined together to help move my stuff in from the car and start to unpack a bit. I knew I wanted to take some time to get things just where I wanted, so you and mom backed off and gave me my space and time to adjust. That really worked for me and gave me some great bonding time with floor mates."

"Was there any part of getting started and settled that didn't work well for you at college?" I asked, remembering some of the phone calls that happened shortly after we left her to return home.

"Oh yeah," she said in a much calmer tone now than those years ago. "I wasn't sure what the classes were and the expectations. I was really nervous that I was off base – maybe didn't belong there. In hindsight, I think that was mostly just that I was starting something new, felt a little homesick, and hadn't yet made real connections with people. It didn't last long, but it's something I should remember when Sue starts. I've got to help her meet people and get quickly acclimated. And, I've also got to give her time to settle in before I expect too much from her."

"Great, let's go to more memories you have of when you started different jobs. What else is coming up for you?"

"Oh my! I just flashed back on sitting in a small office by myself having to complete tons of paperwork. Sure, they had my application and resume, and all that. But now I had to once again fill in all kinds of forms – stuff like selecting a health coverage plan, emergency contact information, whether I wanted to participate in profit sharing and how I'd like my contributions invested. They gave me an employee handbook filled with policies, regulations, something called progressive discipline process – so much information – and they told me to read it and sign that I had received a copy." She sighed. "I know all that is necessary, but it felt rushed and nobody seemed to feel it was very important, just routine. And again – you know me. I don't like to sign something until I've read it thoroughly and had a chance to ask questions."

"So what does that suggest about how to handle that with

What Does It Mean To Be A Manager?

Sue?" I wondered.

"HR will do all that – but I'm going to be sure they give her ample time to review and ask questions. It may be routine for us, but some of it may be new to Sue."

"What else?"

"Let's see. I remember wondering who I'd be working with. I'd met some as a 'meet and greet' or more detailed interview during my candidating. But now that I was officially a part of the organization, I was looking forward to getting to know them better. The team I was assigned to took me out to lunch the first day so I had a chance to put names with faces. But it was a bit overwhelming. I was curious to learn more about each person's background, how long they'd been with the organization, what their job was, and of course – since at that time it was all about me – how'd they be working with me. So, before you ask, I need to work with my current team to plan a welcome lunch but also a way to help her get to know each one individually over the first few days or weeks. One thing they should discuss is how they might work together."

"What –" I started to ask.

Ariel jumped in – "'What else?' you're going to ask. Other things were pretty straightforward. Where was my workspace? What tools did I have to work with – especially a computer with what kinds of software and internet access. Where and when would I be able to get food. And, of course – where was the restroom?"

"And one more thing I remember from my last job. This was great. On my first day, my manager reviewed the job expectations and gave me permission not to do everything right or right away. Earlier, Dad, you referred to the Target Performance Level for a given position. My manager reminded me of what was going to be expected over time and that it would take a bit of time to get there. She also told me that I'd have a fair amount of her time to help me learn the job and to not hesitate to ask questions. She worked with me to put together a bit of a plan of what I would be doing for the first few months as I got up to the level of performance expected. We even went over the kinds of decisions that I would eventually make, but that for the time being, she clarified what I should just decide and do and what things I should pass by her before I took action. Even though I'd had positions before in which I made lots of decisions, this would give me a chance to learn their way of doing things before I just went ahead based on my past experiences and assumptions. Fortunately, I was a quick

What Does It Mean To Be A Manager?

learner and soon the decisions I suggested didn't require that second look – unless they were really big decisions. It helped to know from the get go what my level of authority was – and wasn't."

Ariel paused. "Gosh, there was so much I wanted and needed to know. I can imagine Sue's going to be curious about all those things, too."

"Ariel, you've identified lots of items for a manager to do to initiate a new employee. Let's see if we can make a kind of checklist for providing Sue with a terrific on-boarding process."

I started, "Under the management task of Initiate, I'm going to suggest 12 possible categories of action. They have no required order and some may vary by organization or even by state or federal regulations. To help you remember them, they all start with the letter 'P'.

"Dad, I remember back in elementary school how you taught me to remember things using mnemonic devices" she laughed. "I hadn't understood it when you first said it, so I thought you said 'demonic devices', that somehow the devil was going to be involved. But mnemonic devices have helped me through the years with all kinds of things I've had to recall. Let's hear what you've got."

"OK – and again, in no specific order. Listen to them all then we'll clarify anything you want.

    * Position - reclarifying the work to be done and the general results to be achieved – the performance targets

    * Projects – what specifically the employee will be working on for the first 30-60-90 days

    * Process – the plan for getting up to speed over what period of time

    * People – who the employee will be working with directly as well as who are other stakeholders inside and outside the organization

    * Partner(s) – who specifically, including the boss, will be working with the employee to help her get adjusted – sometimes called a 'buddy'

    * Place – your specific workstation, and also a tour of the facility so the employee knows her way around including places for food and restrooms

    * Provisions – the tools and equipment she'll have access to – from computers and log-ins, to pens, paper, telephones, keys, and how to access any shared resources such as printers, administrative support, meeting spaces

    * Paperwork – all that stuff that needs to be filled in, reviewed, signed and so on

    * Power – what level of authority the employee has to

start with and how that might change over time

And three things I didn't hear you describe from your own experience

    * Publicity – how the organization will notify other employees, customers, vendors, and other stakeholders that the employee is now on board. This is especially evident where someone comes in at an executive level and will interface a lot with people outside the organization.

    * Past, Present and Potential – a conversation about the history of the organization, it's vision and mission, who it serves in what ways, the culture, and so on. This is to help the new employee from outside the organization connect with the context.

    * Probation – often left to the employee to 'discover' in the employee handbook. This is the part where the manager re-ensures the new hire that we're all working together for mutual success. And, it's not an entitlement. We all have to continually earn the right to work here and make a positive difference.

Any of these you want to clarify further?"

"I like that 30-60-90 day concept. What happens at the end of 90 days?"

"In some organizations, they use it as a 'rolling 30-60-90'. After each month, progress is documented for the 30 days just completed, and a new 30 days is added on the back end."

"Good idea. And when that's tied into the strategic plan and the specific goals for the year, it will help each person know what they should be working on and how they're doing." Ariel thought aloud.

"We'll probably come back to that with another task of management sometime in the future." I suggested.

"I also like the idea of a 'buddy' who is not the manager. I wish I'd had someone I could have talked with to get the unvarnished truth without being concerned about job security. And also, it didn't feel right to have to run to my boss to ask where to find extra toner for the copier."

She added, "I also really like the idea of 'Past, Present, and Potential'. I believe it's really important to know where I fit in context. For me, it's not enough to just do a good job. I want to know that what I do matters and that it helps move the organization and our mission forward in a meaningful way."

What Does It Mean To Be A Manager?

"It sounds to me like you've got it. Coupled with your own experiences – good and not so good – this list should give you **P**lenty to **P**urposely **P**lan to **P**romote **P**rogress toward **P**ositive **P**roductivity," I punctuated humorously.

Ariel groaned. "Uh – gee – I have a lot of work to get to. Thanks, Dad. Bye."

COMMUNICATE

Chapter 5: COMMUNICATE

A week later, Ariel and I were on the phone catching up on general news. I shared that I'd just received an email from a CEO client who took action on something that seemed – to me – to not be in his best interest. My client, whose core business was struggling to keep afloat, had just purchased another company. My immediate internal reaction was disappointment that we had not talked first and concern that this purchase could really pull his business down.

"How come that happened, Dad? Don't your clients typically talk these things through with you before they take such a significant step?" asked Ariel.

"Absolutely – but not this time. I've got a lot of assumptions about what happened. Now that I'm a little past my immediate reactions, I want to check my assumptions and better understand his thought process. For all I know at the moment, it may have been a great decision and I just don't know the full story."

"So how are you going to talk to him about this?" she wanted to know. "I get confused by some people's decisions and actions - sometimes my boss and some colleagues; even some friends, rarely. I also feel disappointed that we didn't talk about it and I start making assumptions and judgments about their behavior."

"Ariel, I'd value your thoughts on how I might approach my client." Then, seeing this as a good opportunity to continue our discussion on the tasks of management, I suggested, "Let's talk about the situation using the task I call 'Communicate'. This task starts at the beginning of the employee performance phases and continues throughout the time you are together."

"Sounds like that could work, Dad."

"So, let's back up a moment and consider what we know about general human behavior in any situation. What I want to talk us through is called 'The Ladder of Inference' – originally described by Chris Argyris and I initially learned about it through Peter Senge's *The Fifth Discipline*. It makes a lot of sense to me and I use it whenever I become aware that I think – in my head – that someone has made or will make a poor decision, or I just want to understand more of their reasoning. Of course, there are many more situations when it might be appropriate, but these are the ones that most often trigger me."

"So let's hear it! I'm looking forward to helping *you* figure out what to do."

"OK – think of this as a ladder, the bottom rung of which is reality. This is everything that is happening at any given moment as it could potentially be recorded objectively by video, audio, brain scans, whatever. None of us ever experiences reality as it actually is. In the moment, whatever reality we experience is immediately filtered through the second rung of the ladder, our experience. 'Experience' can be summed up as anything we've been exposed to or engaged with in our life up to that point. It can also include genetics and brain patterns and personality," I started to explain.

What Does It Mean To Be A Manager?

Ariel jumped in. "I get it. Since each individual has had her unique life experience, how she filters what's happening in any given moment is also unique to every person. Right?"

"Yep. The next few rungs on the ladder happen entirely in one's own head, instantaneously and usually subconsciously. We take in our filtered sense of reality, make assumptions about what and why something appears to be the way it is, draw conclusions of what it means, then develop beliefs based on our conclusions. A key thing in these steps is that most of us experience our beliefs as 'right' - what really happened and what to do about it."

"So that's what 'jumping to conclusions' means, huh?" said Ariel.

"Yes, and sometimes they may be the right conclusions – and beliefs – and sometimes they may not be accurate or complete. Whatever they are becomes the basis for our decisions and actions – the top rung of the ladder."

"And those decisions or actions when taken is another piece of 'reality' so the process is never-ending," Ariel suggested.

"Exactly. Again, the middle rungs of the ladder happen almost instantaneously without our even realizing it. Even right now, in this conversation – as good as it is – there are continual internal dialogues we are each having in our own head that bring us to say whatever our next statement will be."

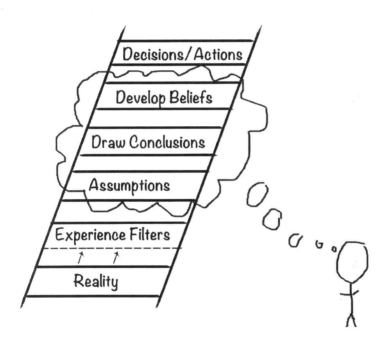

What Does It Mean To Be A Manager?

"Whoa! If that's the way of normal human interaction, are you suggesting we should or could do something different?" Ariel asked.

"What I'm suggesting is that whenever I have a need or desire to more fully understand my own decisions and actions – or those of someone else – such as my client who bought the other business, I can try to slow down the conversation in my head or with the other person. I can ask myself questions like 'How might my life experiences be causing me to filter reality in this moment? What assumptions am I making about what's actually happening and why? What conclusions am I drawing on my possibly inaccurate assumptions? As a result of my conclusions, what do I believe about this situation that I experience as being right – although it may not be?'"

"That's a lot of heady stuff. Is it really necessary?" Ariel queried. Even though we were on the phone, I could sense her eyes rolling.

"It's useful when significant decisions or actions may result – and it's important to try to make the best decision."

"So, this ladder of inference is constant and continual. And it's happening with both people in the conversation all the time – mostly under the radar. If you need to make a joint decision, how do you uncover all that's going on without getting so bogged down that nothing gets done? That would be extremely frustrating to me!"

"Ariel, I believe your life experiences are showing," I laughed. After a pause, "There are a number of ways to use this ladder of inference tool to help with decision making. I find it helpful to call a 'time out' and acknowledge that *I* may be climbing my ladder of inference. I own my part in the conversation. So then I ask or simply offer to make my internal dialogue more visible to each of us by articulating whatever filters, assumptions, conclusions or beliefs I'm aware of in my own thinking. I usually also invite the other person to share his or her ladder. This slows down the conversation, but the additional clarity and insights more often than not lead to a better decision. By slowing down, we actually may go faster because we avoid mistakes and do-overs."

"So – in summary – slowing down the conversation to mutually examine how each other climbed their ladders of inference can lead to better decision making," Ariel recapped. "That makes sense – so how do you plan to use this to talk to your client?"

What Does It Mean To Be A Manager?

"Thanks for keeping me on track," I acknowledged. "Well, next time we talk, I will bring up my considerations right away and acknowledge that I have a number of assumptions that may be incorrect or incomplete. I'll invite him to tell me more of the story behind his decision by walking up his ladder of inference."

"That sounds easier than I think it is, Dad. It felt to me like that conversation would just be coming out of left field. What's the context?" she prodded.

"Good observation. If I don't provide a context it could feel like a 'whiplash conversation'" I acknowledged.

"What's a 'whiplash conversation', Dad?" she asked.

"Oh, that's how I sometimes refer to a comment that seems out of context to what we were talking about and catches me by surprise. It seems to be coming – as you say - out of left field," I responded. "Let's take a closer look at conversations in general – the process. Ariel, have you ever had someone stop you in the hall or come into your office and just start talking – and you're were wondering 'What's this about?'"

"Yeah, there was no context. I usually figured it out, but sometimes I just had to stop them and ask 'What's this about?'"

"For some conversations, it's ok to just figure it out – especially if it's more social or just touching base. However, whenever it is important – or you assume that it is – and that someone will need to make a decision or take action, you've got to raise the level of mutual listening and understanding, such as by using the ladder of inference. Also sometimes you have to get clear on the context. So, as you said, simply ask something like 'What's this about?' You may also want a sense of how long the conversation might take, degree of importance or urgency, who else should be involved, and so on, so you can mutually decide if and how to have the conversation that already started."

"I know sometimes I've suggested we 'put a bookmark on it' and schedule a time and place to continue, especially if others should also be involved – or if I'm in the middle of something else that's a higher priority."

"Great. So let's consider that you've agreed to have the conversation under optimal circumstances. When you get together, what should be the general agenda for an effective conversation?"

"Well I want to understand more of what the context is and

why we're talking. I want to be sure it's useful and efficient. And I want to be sure when it's over that we agree on what's going to happen next," suggested Ariel.

"That's the Three P's – purpose, process, and payoff! Starting out, you may not know the specifics of the payoff, but there could be an agreement that there will be a decision or some action plan created if a next step is required. I usually say that if some actions should happen, don't leave the conversation without restating and agreeing on who will do what by when."

"So," Ariel prodded, "once we're fairly clear on what and why we're talking, I want to be sure we are listening well to each other. I've had some conversations where it feels like we're each stating our perspectives but were not really taking in the other person's ideas. I'm having the conversation inside my own head, believing I know what the other person is going to say, and am just being patient – usually - to state my point of view or say what I've already decided," Ariel admitted. "We seem to be talking *past* each other rather than *with* each other."

"It's great that you recognize that. It's very normal – for most of us. The challenge is to be aware of that 'already-listening' and to instead be more attentive to what the other person is actually saying and why. You could even make it visible by admitting in the moment to the other person what you just told me. Something like, 'I realize that I'm not listening carefully to you. I'm hearing my own internal dialogue. Please restate your last point so I can be sure I'm hearing what you are saying.'"

"Well I probably wouldn't say it exactly like that, but I get your meaning. And sometimes, I may just say it to myself and start paying closer attention," Ariel responded.

After a pause I asked, "Ariel, how do you know when someone is really listening to you?"

"When we're face-to-face, I can see it in the person's body language. In some cultures, it is inappropriate to look directly at the other person. Someone may indicate she's listening with a hand motion, a nod, or even just a slight raising of her eyebrows. In our culture, Dad, I know you're listening to me when you're looking at me. Your body language seems to be appropriately responding – either by leaning forward with a sense of openness, or even sitting back with arms and legs crossed, but still connected."

"What else?" I prodded.

What Does It Mean To Be A Manager?

"Sometimes you grunt," she said humorously.

"Yeah, I guess I do make some funny noises. And what else?"

"Well, more seriously, you ask questions or make statements that seem to be in the flow of the conversation."

"And what else?"

"Well, periodically you restate or paraphrase what I've said. Sometimes I sense you're checking your own understanding of what I said. Other times when you paraphrase, it seems you're checking to be sure I feel I've been heard. I can tell the difference when you follow up by asking me 'Did I get that right?' or 'Does it sound like I'm hearing you correctly?'"

"Uh huh ..." I prodded.

"Oh yeah, and sometimes you paraphrase because you want to ask a question or add your own comment. It's kinda like you have to earn the right to do that by making sure I felt heard."

"And what kinds of questions do I ask?"

COMMUNICATE

"Often you want more information – so you ask questions like, 'And what else?'" I could sense her 'gotcha' smile. "And lot's of times – usually – it's to encourage me to explore my own thinking – not only what I'm saying, but also why."

"Ariel, you definitely have a good grasp on listening!" I congratulated her.

"Well, I did grow up in our household," she laughed. "And, I've had a lot of training on active listening for the work that I do. I've learned to listen for the facts as well as to pay attention to the emotions and body language given diverse cultural contexts."

"You have a high degree of emotional intelligence'" I acknowledged.

"Thanks Dad. I use a lot of these communication skills, usually unconsciously. Most of the time I'm a pretty good communicator. However, I'm getting the sense that when I'm in a particularly important – or difficult – conversation, I may need to be more conscious about using those natural skills."

"Absolutely!" I affirmed. "And it may help to request the other person use them as well. That could be a direct request to use the skills, or more subtle while taking responsibility for your own communication, such as – 'I'm not sure I said that clearly. Could you tell me what you heard?'"

"Dad," Ariel said after a moment, "this is all well and good. However, it seems like we got away from the situation with your client. I hear the concepts and skills you could use – ladder of inference, paraphrasing, clarifying and confirming understanding, body language and tone. That's all helpful for context. Now, what are you going to do?"

"Oh, you're good, Ariel!" I exclaimed. "You always could keep track of a conversation and make sure we got back to the original purpose."

"Thanks, Dad. So – what are you going to do?" she asked, blocking any further tangents.

"OK. I'm meeting with my client next Wednesday. I'll send him an email to let him know I'd like to better understand his decision and what actions he's going to take moving forward to make this a success – hopefully. Actually, I'll leave out the word 'hopefully' because that's a reflection of my judgment and I don't know enough yet."

"And what else?" she asked in her sincere imitation of my

---

coaching.

"When we meet, and it's time to explore his decision, I'll express that I'm making a number of assumptions that I want to check out to gain more clarity."

"It seems like there's more going on for you…" Ariel encouraged.

"There is. I want to express my concerns that we didn't discuss the opportunity and decision before he made it. I see my role as helping my clients with these kinds of opportunities and potentially tough choices, and was disappointed – even annoyed – that I wasn't included so I could be of possible assistance."

"Wow – 'annoyed'! That's pretty strong."

"It's how I felt – and still feel – especially since it still seems like it may have been a poor decision that could have been avoided," I sighed.

Ariel let me sit with my feelings for a few moments, then gently asked, "How will you handle your feelings when you have the conversation with him? It sounds like your nerve endings are really raw."

What Does It Mean To Be A Manager?

"In my work – for better or worse – I've often chosen to keep my feelings to myself, unless I feel they are important and useful to share. In this case, it's helpful to know what I'm feeling at this moment, but this isn't about me. He owns this decision – not me – and it's my job to help him re-examine his decision-making process and how to move forward now that the decision is made. "

"You still seem to be conflicted about if and how to share your feelings with your client. They seem to be pretty strong. But, for now, I'll go along with your plan – after all – you own that decision. So, what …?" Ariel began.

"Ariel," I said, jumping in. "You know, you're on to something here, and it's probably worth exploring, although a bit uncomfortable for me. At least one important issue is why he didn't include me – or for that matter, other trusted advisors – in this critical decision. And since, as you pointed out, I do have some strong feelings about this, that is a conversation we should have. Beyond the logic and head stuff, we have a relationship. If we are going to have a good one – or a chance for an even better one – we need to be able to talk about this stuff, too."

"OK. So …"

"Well, I still plan to have the first conversation about his decision-making process. I will invite him to walk me up his ladder of inference while I clarify and confirm my understanding. Who knows, I may even come to believe that this was a good decision based on what he knew at the time and his vision for growth. I'll hold that hope for now."

"And then…"

"After that, I'll invite us to have what I call the 'meta-conversation' – the conversation about how we have the conversation and the relationship."

"That sounds like it could be worthwhile, but tough. How do you handle that potential conflict?" Ariel wanted to know.

"Well, first, I want to clarify the word 'conflict'. We all have different dictionaries based on our life experiences. For me, sometimes 'conflict' implies confrontation and a competition to see who wins. In this case, I'd like to use the word 'difference'. I want us to explore our differences regarding the situation."

"I'm not sure I have the same dictionary – but I get your point. I know some people who approach a difference as a competition to see who wins and who loses. Some of them do all they can to win – or at least make sure the other person loses. Some of them just cave in – essentially lose either to avoid the confrontation or to stop it from continuing. Most of the time my role – and that of my co-workers – is to search for compromise – win some, lose some – or, if possible, a win-win situation. That's really hard," Ariel commented.

"Ariel, you've just done a great job summarizing work done by Kenneth Thomas and Ralph Kilmann on conflict modes. They created a model for understanding how people behave when there is a difference in a given situation. On the vertical axis they called 'Assertiveness', they consider the extent from low to high that a person attempts to get what he or she wants. On the horizontal axis, 'Cooperativeness', they consider the extent from low to high that the individual attempts to satisfy the other person. From your own descriptions you can identify five different modes. High assertiveness and low cooperation they call 'Competing'. Low assertiveness and low cooperation is 'Avoiding'. Low assertiveness and high cooperation is 'Accommodating'. Middle assertiveness and middle cooperation is 'Compromising'. And high assertiveness coupled with high cooperation is 'Collaborating'.

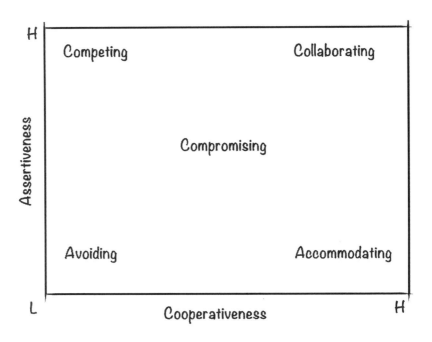

"Well, Thomas and Kilmann were certainly brilliant people," laughed Ariel. "Actually, I'd learned about the model in a Psych class at college. Now it makes a lot more sense to me. So, back to your comment, Dad, about using the word 'difference' rather than 'conflict'. I like that. For some reason 'difference' sounds like it would be more likely to resolve."

"You may be right. Regardless of what we call it, having a difference with another person can be very challenging to get to a win-win. This is done by a sincere effort to collaborate. The skills we've been discussing can help in that effort."

"How so?"

"Well, in the case of my difference with my client, the first thing I want to acknowledge is that we may have a difference. If we don't say something to that effect, it's possible that we'll miss the opportunity to explore it – or one or the other of us may continue to act as if it doesn't exist. In the long run, that can be detrimental to the relationship."

"So, after you both agree that you may have a difference, then what?" Ariel asked.

"Then, we have to work to define the difference. With my client, I have to ask and listen for what is important to him – and why. And I have to express what is important to me – and why. For example – putting words in his mouth based on my current understanding, he may say something like, 'It's important to me to seize an opportunity when it comes along so I can grow my company. In this case, I felt if I didn't say yes to the offer right when I heard about it, I would miss the opportunity.' And I might say, 'It's important to me to help my clients evaluate opportunities so they can make the best decision, and so I feel useful and valuable.'"

"You make it sound simple. I know it can take some work to get you both clear on what's important and why," Ariel suggested.

"Absolutely. But as we do that work, we might likely find we have some commonalities – such as we both want him to grow his business and be successful."

"So, once you've agreed on that, you can use that clarity to explore where you have differences about how to achieve the goals you have in common."

"Exactly – even if we are over-simplifying it. I believe if we at least recognize we want many of the same things, we are now, in a way, on the same side of the table to explore how to make things work for both of us."

"I know you can't predict how the entire conversation will turn out, but it does sound hopeful. If you're working with each other as allies, there's a greater chance to find win-win solutions for moving forward together. I can use that with my co-workers and clients. Thanks, Dad."

"And don't forget to end the conversation with clarity about the next steps of who will do what by when," I reminded us both.

"And," she suggested, "acknowledge the good work you did

together and an appreciation of the effort put into strengthening the relationship."

"You're good! And, thank you for helping me stay honest about expressing my feelings to surface and explore difference."

"Dad, it was good talking to you. I've got a meeting in about half an hour I have to prepare for and all this stuff about effective communication will help us have a more productive session. Thanks. Love you."

"Love you, too. Bye."

ENCULTURATE

Chapter 6: ENCULTURATE

"Hi Dad," Ariel said as I joined the Sunday evening Skype. I listened to and added my own updates to the rest of the family chatter. After the conversations were winding down, Ariel asked if I could stay on the call a bit longer as she had a couple more questions for me about the management task of communication.

"So, what's up, Ariel?" I asked as a segue after the rest of the family exited the conversation.

What Does It Mean To Be A Manager?

"I was looking over my notes from our last conversation and wondering if I missed something. It seems we talked a lot about *how* to communicate, but not so much about *what* to communicate. Given that you said this task runs throughout the performance cycle of the employee, what kinds of things do we actually talk about?" she asked. "I know we'll talk about her job responsibilities and performance over time, and certainly things like client issues and other employees, but I have a sense there are other topics that would be discussed."

"Good observation, Ariel. What might be other topics for on-going discussion?"

"Well, I've been thinking about that. I know you and I have talked before about organizational vision, mission, and values. As a manager, I don't have much influence on defining those, but I have a lot of influence on how we act in accordance with them, especially the values."

"Again, different organizations do things in their own ways. In my experience, vision, mission, and values don't change very often. They were likely in place before you started. Some organizations do periodic reviews along with strategic planning and you may have an opportunity to influence any changes. And I absolutely agree with you that as a manager

---

you have responsibilities to talk about and ensure that your employees' behaviors are in alignment. That's the management task I call 'Enculturate' – and it's another one that runs through the entire performance cycle.

"Dad, I'd like to explore that idea of culture a bit further. Mary, one of my longer-term employees asked me something that got me thinking. She said she knows what her job responsibilities are, the specific tasks she's working on, and who to work with to achieve the expected results. She was wondering about the *how*. Specifically she asked, 'What are the norms for getting things done around here?'"

"What do you think was the reason for her question?"

"I asked her that, wanting to be sure I didn't just race up my ladder of inference. She explained that recently she went to others for help and that most were eager to offer what they could. However, in one case she heard something like, 'That's not my job'. Another example she gave related to a client issue. She asked around and again got different responses ranging from 'Whatever the client needs' to 'We have to manage client expectations in line with our budget.' She said she was confused about how to make decisions in alignment with the values of the organization – specifically those around being collaborative and client focused."

What Does It Mean To Be A Manager?

"And how did you respond to her?"

"I said that there will continue to be situations where our choices are not clear cut. We should review our vision, mission, and values to remember why we exist and how we want to show up in the world. Then, when situations arise that seem to suggest a conflict among the values, we have to talk with others and use our best judgment to determine the best course of action." Ariel sighed. "That just seems so cliché."

"Yes it does, but that doesn't mean it's not a good response." I paused. "You suggested two things I want to explore further. The first is that the organization's values were already agreed to, and, I assume written down somewhere. Is that right?"

"Yes. We have a list – and even some definitions and examples of each one."

"That's great – and more than many organizations. The second thing I picked up on is that there can be situations in which it seems some values may be in conflict with one another."

"Right. Like the example Mary used of being client focused

and fiscally responsible. It seemed confusing as to what value has a higher priority."

"I don't want to get too philosophical, but you've just described a major challenge in the whole of human history! We have multiple groups of people who agree on a set of values – in theory – but who differ on how to act in accordance with them - in practice."

"At the moment, I don't want to get too philosophical either, Dad. So how should I handle this in my workplace?"

"Well, let's start with the proposition that each organization can write and define their values and set priorities in any way they choose. Where the rubber meets the road is what shows up as the cultural norms. As Mary was asking, *how* do things get done around here?"

"OK. So, I should talk with Mary – and others – about the situations that arise and the kinds of choices she makes based on our values, especially when things are not so clear cut. That will help clarify our values in practice, especially if two or more seem in conflict."

"Exactly. Look for opportunities to reinforce behaviors that are in concert with the espoused values and cultural norms. "

What Does It Mean To Be A Manager?

"I can see that many of our values and cultural norms will guide behavior, and that if there are times when things are not obvious, we can talk them through based on the specifics of the given situation."

"Sounds like a plan. Let me ask you this - are there any values and cultural norms that seem to stand without question? This is often demonstrated by the organization's response when someone acts contrary to an espoused value."

"Interesting question. From what I've seen here so far, there are almost always exceptions to the rules – or values and norms. I can think of two situations where I heard that someone was terminated for acting contrary to our values. One was a few years ago when one employee was yelling at and threatening another employee. In the organization's explanation for the termination, they emphasized that the employee acted contrary to the value of mutual caring and safety. I'm sure there was more to the story, but that's what I heard about shortly after I started." I could sense she was remembering the story and gave her a moment.

"And the other one?"

"We have a value of integrity in all that we do. A few months ago, an employee was terminated for telling a reporter some proprietary information. That put our organization in jeopardy, not because we were doing anything wrong, but because our policy is that client information is confidential. That employee betrayed the client's and the organization's trust."

"Wow! Trust is an important value in any organization – or any relationship for that matter. It's often one of those words with many different dictionaries. I'd like to explore that further – both to help you be clearer on what it means to you and to model one way of communicating with Mary and others about values and norms."

"OK. I *trust* this will be useful," Ariel suggested with a smile in her voice.

"Ha ha! Ariel, that's as bad as my puns. So, seriously, what do you mean when you say you trust someone?"

"That she is honest. She doesn't lie to me, but always tells the truth."

"OK. What else might you mean when you say you trust her?"

"That she has a positive intention. She means well and wants to do the right thing."

"OK. And what else?"

"That she has the ability to produce the required results."

"Great. So beyond honesty, we have two additional meanings of trust - positive intention and ability. Do they always happen together?"

"No. There are people I trust because of their positive intentions, but who don't necessarily have the ability. They'll give something their best shot, but it doesn't always get us what we need. And I have others with knowledge and skills that can get results, but who don't always put forth the effort."

"So you've identified three kinds – or perhaps building blocks - of trust so far. The person tells you the truth. That she has positive intention and/or the ability to get results."

ENCULTURATE

Ability to Produce Results: Has the knowledge and skills needed.
Positive Intention: Means well. Wants to do the right thing.
Honesty: Tells me the truth. Doesn't lie.

I continued, "So, what else might you mean when you say you trust someone?"

"If I trust that someone is honest, has both the ability and the desire to get results, I trust her even more if she gets those results consistently. I trust her to keep doing the things that work. She demonstrates commitment. And, that gives me more trust because now I can predict and count on her effort and output."

"Terrific! The jargon is the person talks the talk and walks the walk. I can count on you to do what you say you're going to do."

What Does It Mean To Be A Manager?

Consistency and Predictability: Talks the Talk. Walks the Walk.
Ability to Produce Results: Has the knowledge and skills needed.
Positive Intention: Means well. Wants to do the right thing.
Honesty: Tells me the truth. Doesn't lie.

I continued. "OK. You've moved from what I call 'transactional trust' to 'relationship trust'."

"What do you mean by that, Dad?"

"Transactional trust occurs in any one-time interaction. What's at stake is the outcome of that single interaction. So the degree of honesty, desire and ability are specific to the situation. When you have continued interactions with the same person, what's at stake transitions to – or at least includes – the outcomes of the relationship. So, when you suggest consistency and predictability, you're starting to consider multiple interactions and the development of relationship trust."

"I see," responded Ariel. "If my intent is to build a positive and lasting relationship, there are more blocks of trust to build upon."

"Absolutely. So, continuing with relationship trust, what else do you mean when you say you trust someone?"

"I remember in college psych we talked about factors that help build relationships – especially emotional bonds. Those included shared experiences, cooperative efforts, and proximity. There were also factors about similarity of personality, gender, ethnicity, language and culture" she thought aloud. "So, when I say I trust someone, I think I'm saying we can relate to each other around what we have in common. Or, for that matter we respect each other's differences, as well."

"So, having things in common and mutual respect may be necessary for another building block of trust.

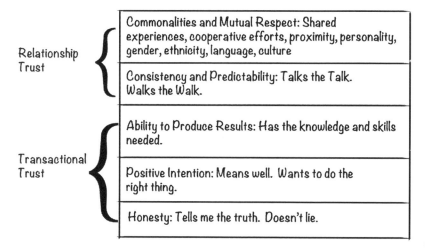

Relationship Trust
- Commonalities and Mutual Respect: Shared experiences, cooperative efforts, proximity, personality, gender, ethnicity, language, culture
- Consistency and Predictability: Talks the Talk. Walks the Walk.

Transactional Trust
- Ability to Produce Results: Has the knowledge and skills needed.
- Positive Intention: Means well. Wants to do the right thing.
- Honesty: Tells me the truth. Doesn't lie.

However, have you had some commonalities with anyone and yet not felt that you can trust that person?"

"Unfortunately yes. So it's got to be something more specific. Hum. I like the mutual respect as well, but I can like and respect someone, and still not trust her. " She paused. "Earlier we were talking about cultural norms as the expression of values in practice. I trust someone who has values similar to mine. I'd know that was the case through those shared experiences about how we each showed up. And, if we have mutual respect, that's another indication of shared values – even if we disagreed about something."

"Block six – shared values. These act as the filters for experience and choices.

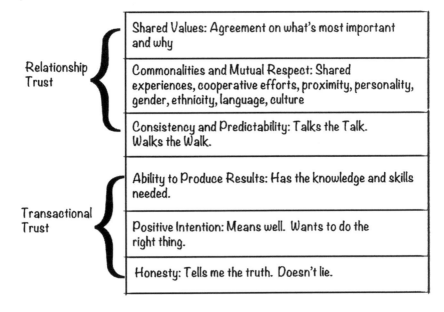

Relationship Trust	Shared Values: Agreement on what's most important and why
	Commonalities and Mutual Respect: Shared experiences, cooperative efforts, proximity, personality, gender, ethnicity, language, culture
	Consistency and Predictability: Talks the Talk. Walks the Walk.
Transactional Trust	Ability to Produce Results: Has the knowledge and skills needed.
	Positive Intention: Means well. Wants to do the right thing.
	Honesty: Tells me the truth. Doesn't lie.

What might come next?"

"Let's see. Someone is honest. She has both positive intent and the knowledge and skills to get things done. Our relationship has grown through demonstration of consistency I can count on. We have a number of commonalities, and most importantly, we have similar values that guide our actions. The next thing is to make the right stuff happen. We'd have to have common goals and expectations."

"Ariel, that's great. So a seventh block is common goals.

Relationship Trust	Common Goals and Expectations to make the right stuff happen
	Shared Values: Agreement on what's most important and why
	Commonalities and Mutual Respect: Shared experiences, cooperative efforts, proximity, personality, gender, ethnicity, language, culture
	Consistency and Predictability: Talks the Talk. Walks the Walk.
Transactional Trust	Ability to Produce Results: Has the knowledge and skills needed.
	Positive Intention: Means well. Wants to do the right thing.
	Honesty: Tells me the truth. Doesn't lie.

What Does It Mean To Be A Manager?

Keep going – what else?"

"I guess, for me, the ultimate proof of trust is that someone's got my back."

"What's that mean?"

"That even if I'm not present, she will act in my best interests based on our common values and goals. She would likely be making the same decisions I would make, or at least consider what I might ask and do if I were there. And, I guess, even more so, she'll do everything she can to make sure no harm comes to me or the organization in my absence."

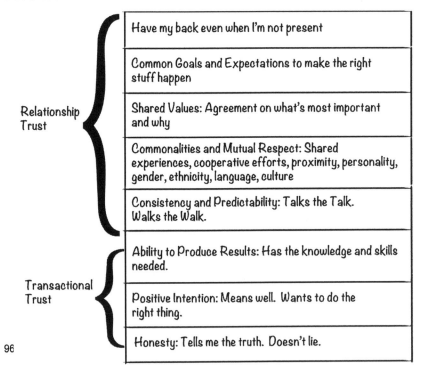

Relationship Trust

- Have my back even when I'm not present
- Common Goals and Expectations to make the right stuff happen
- Shared Values: Agreement on what's most important and why
- Commonalities and Mutual Respect: Shared experiences, cooperative efforts, proximity, personality, gender, ethnicity, language, culture
- Consistency and Predictability: Talks the Talk. Walks the Walk.

Transactional Trust

- Ability to Produce Results: Has the knowledge and skills needed.
- Positive Intention: Means well. Wants to do the right thing.
- Honesty: Tells me the truth. Doesn't lie.

ENCULTURATE

"Wonderful. Anything else?"

"Not that I can think of."

"I'll add one more. Reciprocity. She's got my back *and* I have hers. For me, it brings up the concept of integrity. Wholeness, unification, indivisible. All the parts are interconnected and we act as one."

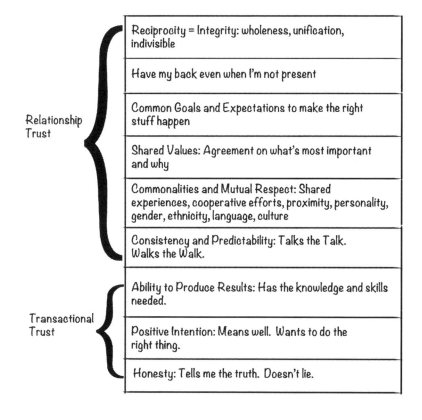

Relationship Trust

- Reciprocity = Integrity: wholeness, unification, indivisible
- Have my back even when I'm not present
- Common Goals and Expectations to make the right stuff happen
- Shared Values: Agreement on what's most important and why
- Commonalities and Mutual Respect: Shared experiences, cooperative efforts, proximity, personality, gender, ethnicity, language, culture
- Consistency and Predictability: Talks the Talk. Walks the Walk.

Transactional Trust

- Ability to Produce Results: Has the knowledge and skills needed.
- Positive Intention: Means well. Wants to do the right thing.
- Honesty: Tells me the truth. Doesn't lie.

What Does It Mean To Be A Manager?

"Interesting. 'Integrity in everything we do' is one of our organization values. I have a new and deeper appreciation of what that really means."

"Ariel, integrity is the highest level of trust for me. It goes beyond me asking who do I trust and helps me ask if I am worthy of their trust as well."

"Gee, is that all there is?" Ariel joked.

"It's a beginning," I laughed back. "Remember, when we started this conversation, you were wondering what to talk about over time with employees. This is some of that content. Further, we wanted to explore one way to talk about values and norms. You were also wondering how to handle situations in which two values seem at odds with one another – such as the balance between providing what a client needs and managing expectations within the budget. What are your thoughts on this, now?"

"Well, as I look over my notes from this conversation, I can see there are multiple building blocks as a part of trust. There is not necessarily a single hierarchy or sequence. For example, are shared values more important than common goals? And which comes first? So, my take away is that regarding any given value – or whenever values seem to be in conflict – what's most important is to talk it through given the specifics of the transaction and the desire for a longer-term positive relationship."

"That's a very good perspective."

"This was very helpful – and thought provoking. I like the idea of taking each one of our espoused values and helping us think through what it really means and how it shows up in the workplace. Sue starts tomorrow. I'll be sure to include the enculturate task along with the initiate task. I can also see these discussions being helpful for outside-of-work relationships. I know it's given me a lot I want to talk about with my significant other and get his ideas as well. Thanks, Dad. Love you – and I know what 'love' means when I say it."

Thanks, Ariel. I love you, too. Bye."

Chapter 7: MOTIVATE

A week later, Ariel and I were talking by Skype and catching up on all the personal stuff. I shared how much I was enjoying playing in the classical guitar ensemble this semester and that her Mom and I had had a wonderful weekend at our cottage in Michigan. We had particularly relished the walk in the autumn woods over the long-ago sand dunes bordering Lake Michigan. There were so many forks in the deep-woods paths that I had to use the GPS on my smart phone to be sure we could find our way to the bluffs overlooking the lake and then find our way back to where we'd parked our car. There were times I couldn't get

_____

a clear signal and we had to take our best guess, a bit of a risk as it was nearing dusk.

Ariel had a number of things to update us on as well. The state fair was coming to town and she was looking forward to seeing the ginormous vegetables on display – especially the pumpkins, the exhibits of products made in the state, and of course the hawkers shouting, "It slices! It dices!" as they demonstrated their latest kitchen gadgets.

"So, how's it going with Sue this last week?" I asked, remembering that Sue would have started last Monday.

"Great. We're off to a good start. She's doing exactly what we need her to do and is making suggestions for ways to improve some aspects of her role and the organization. Some of her suggestions are right on, but we need a bit more time and other resources before we can implement anything. She seemed a little frustrated that we can't just wave a magic wand and make everything perfect. Actually, she reminds me of me. However, seeing it in her also reminds me that a couple times, shortly after I started this job, I was feeling that kind of frustration and was wondering if I'd made the right choice. I wonder if she's feeling any of that?"

What Does It Mean To Be A Manager?

"I think that's a very normal feeling. It may come sooner or later to anyone, and we often speak of it as, 'The honeymoon is over'."

"Well, I think it's way too soon to worry about it. She'll probably settle in to a good rhythm and be successful. As I said before, she's got the right skill set, a good set of values that align with the organization, and a personal style that fits in with the culture inside the organization and with our clients. I'll just keep my eye on it."

"Ariel, that's what most managers do – kind of keep an eye on it. Some just ignore it, figuring if and when there's an issue with a person's performance, they'll deal with it then. I believe another crucial task of a manager that continues throughout all employee performance phases is what I call 'Motivate'. However – I don't mean 'motivate' in the way many people use the term – to inspire, pump up, and cheer on the employee."

"That's what I thought it means. How are you defining it, Dad?" she asked.

"I think every employee wants to be a part of something significant that makes a positive difference to another person or situation. They do this while working with and for others as long as they feel they are able to make that contribution – or until something else attracts them to a different opportunity for significance."

"Whoa! I thought employees are *only* looking for a way to make money and improve their own life conditions," interrupted Ariel sarcastically.

"Well, actually, that's true for some," I replied. "But think about it for a moment. What's the value of money to someone?"

"I guess it could be a kind of scorecard that shows someone how well she's doing," Ariel suggested.

"Yes – there are people who want to show their pay stub or bank balance to others. What else?"

"It's not really their bank balance, but what they spend their money on, I think."

"And what do they spend their money on?"

"That varies depending on their values and life context. For some it's the basics like food, shelter, clothing for themselves or their family. If there is money beyond those basics, they may spend it on more of those things, or things like transportation, recreation, education – those kinds of things. Maybe they set some aside for saving for a rainy day or something special. And some, no matter how much they may have, are committed to donating a portion of it to help others," Ariel suggested.

"A great list off the top of your head. And, I think very accurate. So, it's not necessarily about the money, but how a person chooses to use it that seems more important to informing the manager about what matters to the employee."

"Sure – if it's enough money to do those things."

"How much is enough will depend on a person's values and aspirations. One could argue that there's never enough - - or that there is always enough. What I'd like to explore with you is what, besides money, might cause an employee to work in your organization – and what might cause them to leave, as eventually most will do."

"OK. Besides money", she said, "someone might be drawn by the mission. I know I was. Or it could be they are drawn to the people and the culture they get to work with. Or they could be thinking about their opportunity to learn and be challenged. Or they're looking for variety. There are so many things it could be", she said, sounding a bit exacerbated.

"Exactly!" I replied. "Do you think it would help you be a better manager and Sue a better employee if you had some sense of her reason for wanting to work here – besides the money?"

"Of course. And some of that came out during the interviewing process. She wants to support the mission and to continue learning. Eventually she wants to move into management to have more opportunity to lead the organization's work and to effect change in the system at the root level of causes of social problems. Kinda like me."

"For you – and for her - do you believe this organization will provide you with those opportunities forever?"

"Of course not. I hope it will for a long time, but I don't think I'll remain here for the rest of my working life. And, as you know, I've been planning to go to grad school in a few years – once I figure out which of my many interests to pursue."

"So, for a while, as long as your path intersects with the direction of the organization, you share the journey. And at some time in the future, your path will veer off in a different direction while the organization moves along it's own, but now separate path. Right?"

"Yes. My employment here – and Sue's too, I guess – is only temporary - only as long as our paths intersect. I think I understand."

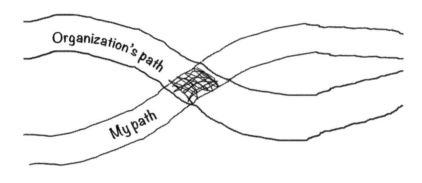

"Let me share another model I've been working on related to someone's possible life journey. It's a pyramid like Maslow's Hierarchy of Needs with an ever-increasing sense of significance and a belief that what I do matters. At the most basic level – analogous to Maslow's physiological survival needs – is that I have something to do and am doing something, even if it's just to stay alive."

"That makes sense from what I remember of Maslow," Ariel encouraged.

"The next level considers that I receive some kind of compensation – money or other benefits - that is enough to meet my basic needs. Of course how much is 'enough' may vary for different people in different circumstances. That corresponds to Maslow's needs for safety and security. The third level indicates a connection to the social and cultural context of what I'm doing – essentially who I'm working with and our norms of engagement."

"I can see that connection to Maslow's need to belong. So next is Maslow's need for esteem and respect, right?" asked Ariel.

"Right. Maslow described it as a need to be valued by oneself and others. I've altered that slightly in my model suggesting that my self-respect and that from others will be partly based on my being productive and achieving intentional results in what I'm doing."

"Are you suggesting in your model, that someone only gets respect by being productive and achieving intentional results? I don't quite agree with that," Ariel stated. "I believe a person is deserving of love and respect from the very onset of their life."

What Does It Mean To Be A Manager?

"Ariel, I agree with you. However, we may be looking at a model too simply. Here I use the analogy of musical scales. Think in octaves. At birth and for the rest of our lives, we are all on a journey. What each of these levels mean – or Maslow's for that matter – depends on where a person is in their life. Octave 1 may include philosophies and practices about basic human rights, including the right to have a life, be provided for by others until able to acquire 'compensation' from one's own efforts, and to have a connection with others with a sense of belonging. Octave 2 and subsequent octaves, continue to recapitulate – or repeat from the beginning – just at higher levels. In my experience, by the time I was about 4 years old, I have been on a more self-aware journey and understood the need to be productive and get intentional results. What's changed for me over time are the results I've intended to achieve."

"I get it," said Ariel. "I want to think about that concept further, but not at the moment. Can we get back to how I can use all this to motivate Sue?"

"Absolutely – but first, one more level, what Maslow called self-actualization. He defined that level as a person's need to achieve their full potential no matter whether expressed by one's profession, avocational pursuits, spiritual development, or whatever. My model suggests that the career path of significance that I'm on through the work I do should help me to learn about who I am in the world, to make my life meaningful."

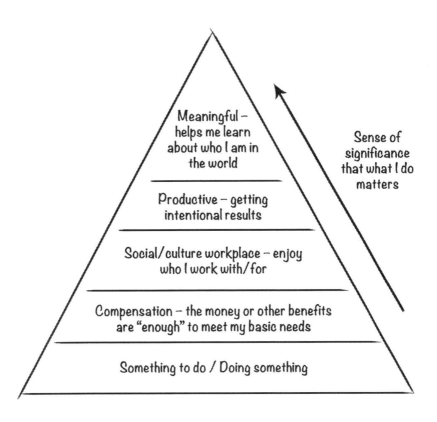

What Does It Mean To Be A Manager?

"I like this model," Ariel responded. "Let me summarize to be sure I've got it and how it could help motivate Sue. First, I understand that she is on her life's journey – part of which includes the work she does. Also, our organization is on a journey as defined by our vision, mission, values, strategy and goals. For some period of time, Sue's path and the organization's path overlap, and each is served by the other to move forward in their respective journeys. Given the hierarchy, Sue needs to be doing something and getting sufficient compensation for her chosen life style. I believe she and we have met those needs for now. Next she would need to work in a social context where she feels a sense of belonging with the people and organization culture. I think that is also being met. So next she has to be productive and achieve intentional results. We're getting there pretty well with the goals we've defined and the training she's received, so she's getting the results the organization needs. So the question might be, is she getting what she needs to have more meaning in her life, to learn about her place in the world, and have a strong sense that what she's doing really matters." Ariel let out a deep breath. "That's a lot!"

"It certainly is, and I think you've summarized it quite well."

"Dad, as much as I agree with this model, it feels like it's way too philosophical to discuss with Sue. I can just imagine her eyes glazing over. How do I use all this to motivate Sue?"

"You're probably right. I suggest the same could be said of Maslow's Hierarchy. However, what we've discussed can serve as a context from which you can determine what kinds of things to discuss with her. You need to understand – and continue to discuss - what's important to Sue and help her connect the dots -- how, by doing what you and the organization ask of her, she will also get what she wants - at least for a while as the paths intersect. The manager's task to motivate is to help the employee discover and make those connections."

"Given that Sue and I had some of these conversations during the interview process, I think we both see the connections. Some others have been around longer – some pre-dating me. I'm not sure that clarity of connection is there for some of them," Ariel thought out loud. "I'm guessing that this is a conversation the manager should have with each employee periodically to keep the connection so they have the desire to do the work we ask of them. How do I bring up this kind of conversation with someone if we haven't had it before?"

"Your thoughts" I prodded.

What Does It Mean To Be A Manager?

"Just ask. Perhaps – "Why do you work here?""

"It could be that simple and direct – although watch out for the word 'Why?' Depending on tone or the person's interpretation, it could come across as needing to justify or defend oneself. Do you have another suggestion?"

"How about – 'What's important to you in your life that working here helps you do, have or be?' I remember 'do, have, be' from a conversation we had a long time ago about want I wanted for my future self. You asked me to visualize my life 10 years from then and I had to answer three different questions – 'What do I want to do?' 'What do I want to have?', and 'Who do I want to be?' I'm still amazed at how each of those questions brought up different responses and how they all needed to work together."

"That's great. You can invite each employee to do a similar exercise. It will be very insightful for them, and to the extent that they share it with you, you will be much clearer about how to motivate them – to help them make the connection between what they want to do, have and be and how they can achieve some of those things by working with you and the organization."

"What if I think their answers are not going deep enough to

give them a sense of direction in their life?" she asked hesitantly. "I mean, I don't feel I should judge them, but sometimes people just go with the first thing that comes to mind."

"You could set up the conversation explaining the 5-Whys process. Again, be careful with the word 'Why?'. Essentially, when someone responds to you – or just herself – what it is she wants to do, have, or be – keep a neutral face and tone. Simply ask something like 'Why is that important to you?' or 'If you do that, what would that mean to you?' or 'How would having that make you feel?' You'll do that at least 5 times, each time evoking a deeper response. The critical aspects of the process are to be curious and non-judgmental. You're working with them as a thought partner not a problem solver."

"No one at this job has ever done that with me. I kind of just take care of it myself. Maybe they assume they know the answers, don't care, or don't think it's appropriate to ask. "

"Would it make a difference for you to have that conversation – especially as you started a job and as you continued doing it?"

"Absolutely! I might stay longer – or leave earlier. I would be frequently reminded about my choice to be there and do that work."

"Exactly. And the word 'choice' is crucial to the conversation. When done well, the employee knows it is a choice – that she has options. When she choses to stay because it helps her get what she wants to do, have, and be, enjoyment and productivity both increase."

"So," summarized Ariel, "the manager's task is to motivate employees by helping each of them gain deeper clarity about what they want to do, have, and be in their life and to connect that to the work I'm asking them to do. And this is not just with new employees, but with each of them over the duration of their employment. Got it. Thanks Dad."

EDUCATE

Chapter 8: EDUCATE

It was only a few days later that I received another call from Ariel. She said she just wanted to go over a few things.

"Sue's been here about a week and I feel I've done a good job on the tasks of initiate, communicate, enculturate, and motivate so far. I recognize that she's just started the training phase of performance, and I'm wondering what else I should be doing to help her get up to the target performance level. Got anything for me?"

What Does It Mean To Be A Manager?

"Of course I do," I laughed. "And you've got lots of stuff for yourself. Let's call this task 'Educate'. This task includes what the manager should do to ensure the employee learns the knowledge and skills they need to do the work – to get up to speed, so to speak – in order to achieve the mutually agreed upon SMART goals."

"Essentially 'training' – right?" said Ariel, cutting to the chase.

"Yes – which is different from – but often overlaps - the initiate task we discussed not too long ago. What have you done so far and how's it working?" I asked.

"Well – you're right in that I started training Sue pretty much as we were doing the orientation tasks. First, we reviewed what her SMART goals would be and what would be – as we said before - the necessary, relevant and sufficient knowledge and skills she would need to use to be successful in achieving those goals. After we identified that knowledge and skills, I had her do a kind of high-level self assessment of her abilities so we could determine what she might need training on," Ariel explained.

"And what did you both find out from that?" I asked.

"It reaffirmed that part of the reason I hired her is that she already had experience doing some similar work. She knew a lot about what procedures were required by government regulations no matter what organization you worked in. And she had a lot of basic computer skills with Word and Excel. We also agreed that our organization had a few other procedures that we needed to bring her up to speed on and that we had some proprietary software programs that generated a variety of unique reports. We would have to teach her all those things. We then put together a plan of what she'd be trained on, by when and by whom – because it wasn't always me doing the training."

"That sounds like a great start. How's it been going?" I wanted to know.

"For the most part really good. She's been learning our procedures and can generate most of the reports already. She's quickly moving up her learning curve toward the target performance level," Ariel responded with the sound of pride in her voice.

"Terrific. And how have you let her know that you are pleased with her progress?" I asked.

"A couple times I told her she's doing a great job. She always smiled and said 'thank you for saying so'. Although, now that I think of it, there were a couple of times she seemed either confused or relieved when I mentioned it."

"Ah ha!" I exclaimed, as I had been partially listening for where I might have some ideas or tips that could be helpful. "Telling someone she is doing a good job – giving that pat on the back – is exactly right to continue to reinforce performance and to ensure you're building a positive relationship. Sometimes it helps to be more specific. For example, when you want to point out a specific result that was achieved or to reinforce a particular behavior or characteristic so Sue gets more clarity on what she's doing right."

Ariel said, "That sounds like a good idea. I'm sure you have a model for how to do that." I could hear the smile in her voice.

"Well, it just so happens that I do. There are three parts to powerful positive reinforcement feedback. The three parts can be in any order, but when all three are included, it's very strong. Here they are – 1) what specific results Sue achieved; 2) what and who benefitted from her achievement, and 3) what behavior or characteristic she demonstrated that enabled her to get those results and benefits." I paused – "Pretend I'm Sue and give me some real-world positive

EDUCATE

reinforcement for something I recently accomplished."

"OK – a bit of role play, then - although I'd guess we could call it real-play because this just happened this week." She started, "Sue, thank you for the great job you did on the Johnson case report. You laid out all the facts and recommendations in a way that makes it possible for the attorneys to quickly absorb the information and sift through the evidence as they prepare for the hearing. Your attention to detail – and meeting deadlines – is really terrific." She paused. "How was that?"

"Excellent! You had all three parts and they flowed together well. How do you think Sue will respond when you say it to her?"

"She'll be really pleased that I tuned in to what she was working so hard to get done and happy that it will serve the client well."

"And – that third part – about her attention to details and meeting deadlines…?"

"She'll appreciate that as well, and she'll know what kinds of behaviors I value. I'm sure she'll continue to focus on those two behaviors on other tasks."

What Does It Mean To Be A Manager?

"OK. One more time just to show that you can say the same thing in any order. Let's hear it," I suggested.

"Sue, I really appreciate your attention to detail and ability to meet deadlines. On the Johnson case report, you did a great job laying out all the facts and recommendations. I'm sure the attorneys will be able to quickly absorb the information and sift through the evidence as they prepare for the hearing."

"Great," I started to say.

Ariel jumped in. "Or – Sue, you've made it easy for the attorneys on the Johnson case to prepare for the hearing. Your attention to detail helped you lay out all the facts and recommendations by the deadline. Great job! Or – Sue, … " she started.

"Ariel – you got it! Your ability to recognize and appreciate Sue's good work with this level of specificity will help her continue to be diligent with details and deadlines. That will help you and the entire staff continue to achieve important results."

"Dad," Ariel asked with a thoughtful tone. "As good as this all sounds, it seems like a lot to say every time Sue does something. I'm concerned it may lose its impact if used too much."

"I agree. What's your own response to that concern?"

"It depends on the person and the situation. I think there are times that Sue would really want to hear the entire message to recognize that I'm paying attention and that what she does matters and is appreciated. I also think – if I do this often enough – that many times just saying 'thank you' will be sufficient."

"Remember, you're in the educate task of management. One of the things psychologists have learned about any kind of training – especially with a new skill - is that more frequent specific positive reinforcement at the beginning anchors the behavior. After it's anchored, the feedback can be less frequent and more intermittent and have a similar effect. And every once in a while, the full three-part feedback will serve to re-anchor the positive behaviors you desire."

"Thanks, that helps. Now, one more thing. As I've been training Sue, there have been a few times that I've had to correct her. Nothing major – yet – but what are the tools for giving corrective feedback?"

What Does It Mean To Be A Manager?

"What have you done so far, and how has that worked?"

"Last week she was on Excel and entered some data in a way that it couldn't be utilized in some of the look-up formulas. I found the error as I was reviewing the report and traced it back to what she'd done. I realized that she had made the mistake unintentionally because she hadn't yet been trained on that specific program. I pointed it out to her and we did a quick training so she now knows what to do differently. It was all matter of fact. No blame. All fixed."

"There are a few things I'm hearing in what you said that I'd like to highlight. First – you said she did it unintentionally. For me, this is one of the most important things a manager – or anyone, for that matter – should recognize. I say it this way: '99% of people 99% of the time mean well'. If a mistake was made – or, to refer back to an earlier conversation we had - if we have a difference - the other person is most likely doing what she thinks is right. There was no intention to make my life difficult."

"I certainly agree with that," Ariel responded.

"So, the second thing is to check out what the person intended. With Sue, she may have intended to enter the data in a way she had learned before – or, using her best

---

judgment and experience - to figure out how it should be entered. You seemed to assume her positive intentions, because you chose to point out the error without blame and provide the training and understanding to do it correctly the next time."

"I think I also apologized for not having provided the training before she attempted the task. I owned my part of the error."

"That's good. Many times I have found myself ready to assign blame to someone else only to realize that I am partly at fault as well. Which leads to a third point from your example, if a mistake is made, be sure you're focused on the behavior not the person. In your story, you both acknowledge the way the data was entered was the problem, not that Sue was an idiot or fool to make the mistake."

"I would never suggest anyone was an idiot or a fool!" exclaimed Ariel.

"I believe that about you, Ariel. Yet, there are many managers who seem to leap to blame the person and perhaps even label them – at least in their heads – as 'idiot' or 'fool' or just that the person has a bad attitude."

What Does It Mean To Be A Manager?

I continued, "So, many times, just pointing out the error and clarifying the correction is sufficient. There are times that it also helps to briefly explain why the change is important and necessary. People often will accept the corrective feedback if they know the reasons behind the request, rather than just doing what they were told."

"That sounds like another option where it depends on the person and the situation."

"That's right. I tend toward providing the why behind the correction. I find it reinforces that I heard their good intention, and it creates more understanding to sustain the new behavior. That practice fits real well when the management task is to educate."

"That helps, Dad. But I want to go a little further. Sue is still in the training phase, and I think moving quickly toward sustaining; that is, she's almost up her full learning curve toward the target performance level. There have been couple times so far, and I expect there will be more, when I think I need to go further with the corrective feedback." Ariel paused to collect her thoughts. "Here's one example. It came to my attention that Sue was working on a project on her own that would be appropriate to collaborate with her colleagues to get their input as well as the fact that whatever

---

actions would come out of her work would have an impact on others. Three things to keep in mind: first, she's done this kind of work elsewhere and was quite competent to do it on her own. Second: I'm working hard to encourage a collaborative culture and her actions make it hard for others to try to work with her. Third: Sue and I have talked about this before – including the why aspects of my request to change her actions. It seems more complex to me because it's not about the work product per se, but about the culture. So, how do I give corrective feedback to keep her doing good work *and* to be more collaborative?"

"Ariel, this level of corrective feedback is part of the educate task for sure – you are helping her learn the skills and knowledge to get the job done and also to learn the norms of what it takes to be successful on your team. The good news is that from your description of the situation, I think you have many of the pieces already in place."

"That's good to hear. How do I talk to her about this?"

"The first thing I noted is that you've discussed it before and the desire for her to be more collaborative didn't seem to stick."

"At least in this instance," Ariel clarified.

What Does It Mean To Be A Manager?

"So, when you talk with her, lay out the context of what you want to talk about and why. Give a <u>brief</u> specific and recent example of the behavior you're concerned about. Then invite her to respond with her perspective – intentions and actions. As she's telling her story – walking up her ladder of inference – use active listening to clarify and confirm your understanding. Then ..."

"Hold it a moment. Let me try it. 'Sue, I want to talk to you about the Sampson project. The work product was very good, but I'm concerned about your process, which did not include others on the team. We've talked about this before. Help me understand how you approached this assignment and your thinking about including others in the process,'" Ariel practiced. "Like that?"

"Very good. Brief and to the point – and it included the invitation to hear her perspective. One little tweak – take out the word 'but'. It can signal that what follows is what's really important and to ignore the rest. You could change it to 'and' or simply leave it out by starting a new sentence."

"Are you saying I should 'but out'?" Ariel laughed. "That would be as bad as one of your puns."

"OK – moving right along..." I snickered. "It was also good

that you reminded her of previous conversations. This will help justify going deeper with your feedback. And I liked your invitation for her to share her thought process. Now, again you'll listen carefully to what she says about what and why she did what she did. Depending on how that goes, if you still feel she needs to change something, you can first reinforce what she did well – or at least her good intentions – then state what you want her to do different."

"So based on what I assume her responses might be – 'Sue, I appreciate that you know how to get the work done and you don't want to unnecessarily take other people's time. Given that we are a collaborative team, I want you to at least check in with others so they know what you are working on and have a chance to give any input they might offer.' How's that?"

"You make it sound so easy. And sometimes it will be. And sometimes it may take a lot of back and forth for you to come to an agreement for moving forward."

"And like we discussed before, the conversation isn't over til we've agreed exactly on who will do what by when."

"Exactly. Personally I'd want to hear it in Sue's own words saying what she's committed to rather than you just restating what you've already said. She'll be more likely to internalize it and take ownership when she hears the commitment in her own voice."

"Sounds good. And I'll watch what happens for a while to hopefully have an opportunity for positive reinforcement. Or determine if we need to talk again."

"I believe you've got it! I'm sure you will have many more opportunities for both positive reinforcement and corrective feedback as Sue moves from training to sustaining her performance."

"Thanks Dad. This was helpful. I'll talk to you and Mom this weekend. Bye for now."

PARTICIPATE

Chapter 9: PARTICIPATE

I was sitting in my office catching up on some office work when my computer beeped indicating I'd received an email. I smiled as I read the subject line from Ariel – "HELP! What do I say now?"

Her email explained that Sue is doing a great job at the target performance level and working well with others. "I give her lots of positive reinforcement and occasional corrective feedback and we talk generally about how things are going. But I wonder, is that enough? What else should I be doing? What else should we be talking about? Or should

What Does It Mean To Be A Manager?

I just stay out of the way and let her do her job?"

I considered that this could be a more-involved conversation and that email was not my preferred way to have the discussion. I sent her an email to that effect and asked her when she'd have about 15 minutes for a phone conversation? She said she'd call me in 20 minutes if that would work for me. We agreed and I started to consider what questions I might ask and – based on only a little information – what I thought would be some tips I might offer.

When Ariel called me, we exchanged a few pleasantries, then she dove right in. "For Sue, and all my other employees, I guess the most important thing they want to hear is how they and we are doing. 'How is my work going? Am I making a difference in the success of the organization and our clients? What else could I or should I be doing?' That kind of stuff."

"You are in the management task I call 'Participate'. As you'll recall, communicate, enculturate, and motivate are on-going through the performance phases. Sometimes they are about the work, but many times they are about the whole person and even may have nothing to do with the tasks at hand. Participate is often more specific and focused on the work – the results to be achieved."

PARTICIPATE

"Ok. So how do I respond to their questions? I'm concerned about how to make sure that we have a useful conversation. I've had those kinds of conversations with my boss where I actually left frustrated, feeling that he didn't listen or understand – or perhaps I didn't listen or understand. I left feeling like I sincerely asked for feedback or direction, and got only platitudes – 'You're doing fine' and 'Keep up the good work' – or just more directives."

"That's a very appropriate concern. Let's first treat these questions as rational, fact seeking. Later, we'll look at them again from an emotional point of view that may sometimes be behind the questions. So, if straightforward fact seeking, where would you get that kind of information?"

"The organization has a strategic plan with yearly goals specified. My department has goals that align with the organization. And, back when Sue started – in my initiate task – I clarified her SMART goals that align with the department. For that matter, each employee has her list of goals for the current fiscal year. One thing I could share is my sense of how each of us, the department, and the organization is doing relative to the goals. Would that be something?"

"Absolutely. Most of us like to know how the 'game' is going.

What Does It Mean To Be A Manager?

I remember years ago you really enjoyed bowling. Imagine a scenario where there was an opaque curtain across the alley. You would have rolled the ball down the alley, through the curtain, and possibly heard a lot of noise, but couldn't see what you'd actually accomplished. You wouldn't even know if you needed to bowl a second time in a given frame or which pins were still standing. In a sense, you did the activity of your job – bowling the ball down the alley. But you were blind to the results - whether you had met your goals. And, to continue this scenario, you looked across several lanes to see your co-workers all bowling their balls, but similar curtains prevented you from knowing whether your team was winning the game."

"That would be really frustrating. I like to see my progress and make adjustments so I can do better," exclaimed Ariel. "I can't imagine wanting to keep playing the game if I didn't know how I was doing."

"So, one part of a manager's job is to remove the curtains – or at least make them transparent. "

"I get it. When I communicate – one-to-one or with the whole team, I have to help everyone see the results of their actions and how that is affecting our whole game," Ariel exclaimed. "I can also see that those kinds of discussions give us a chance to make adjustments in what we are doing so we can do even better."

"That's right. Now, while talking with an employee about her results, how might you remove the curtain, or at least make it more transparent? How might you help the employee have a good sense of how she's doing?"

"I'd probably start with a review of what we and she planned to accomplish with respect to our SMART goals. I could provide an overview of everything, but I think she's most interested in feedback on her own stuff."

"OK. Let's stay at a high level, for now. We'll dig into more specifics then about ways to measure progress and continuously achieve desired results. So, at a high level, how might you respond to her question – direct or implied – about how she is doing?"

"Well, I could just tell her, but being around you, I've learned the value of asking her so she has a sense of ownership. I'd start out by asking, 'Sue, overall, how do you think you're doing?' My guess is that she would say pretty good and still wonder. So, maybe more specifically, I might ask, 'Sue, let's look at each of your specific goals and you tell me how well you think you're doing with respect to each one.'"

What Does It Mean To Be A Manager?

"Ariel, that's an excellent process. I've used what I call a 'traffic light check-in'. For each goal, based on what the measurable end result should be, tell me if you're 'green' – on track to achieve the goal as planned, 'yellow' – a bit behind but you know what to do to get back on track, or 'red' – behind and at risk of not achieving the goal or not sure what to do."

"That's a great idea. That should go fairly fast and help her get a good sense of where she is."

"You can go a bit further, depending on her responses. If she says 'green', ask her for one or two comments about what she's done to stay on track. If 'yellow', ask her what's happened that she now feels a bit behind. Then, based on the description of yellow, ask her what ideas she has for getting back on track. If 'red', again ask what's happened to get her behind and what ideas she has to get back on track as you did with 'yellow'. And, ask her where she may need help from you or someone else. "

"Well, I think that would work well for Sue and others. How often should we have that kind of discussion? Just when they ask or more regularly?"

"What's your opinion based on your own experience?"

PARTICIPATE

"When I was newer to the job, or new on a project, I wanted feedback more frequently. Once I got more comfortable, I just kept on task to get the results we were after," Ariel thought aloud. "So, I guess it depends on the person and the situation about how often we talk and about what."

"Years ago, management consultant Ken Blanchard and his team coined the phrase, 'Situational Leadership'. The basics are just what you suggested. It depends on the person and the situation. Blanchard talked about matching one's leadership – or management – style to the ability and desire of the employee in a given situation. As you experienced, when someone is newer to a task they often need training and more frequent feedback. Over time, once they know what they're doing, the conversations switch to less training and more coaching with the nature of the feedback, often including more self-assessment."

"That makes sense. But what about those people – often me included – who know what they're doing and are doing it well? I don't have much need for feedback on some things – but I still want to hear something from time to time."

"At some point, a manager needs to empower an employee to get the job done. This is best when the employee has the ability and desire to figure out what to do and how to do it for the most part. The management style shifts further to agreeing on results and timelines then asking the employee how they plan to achieve the results and what kind of assistance, if any, they need. Most of the participation during the project is in the form of the employee providing a status report such as we talked about with the traffic-light summary."

"OK, so how I participate with an employee will depend on where they are with their ability and desire to do the job, and how I participate with them will be initially training with lots of feedback to eventually just clarifying end results and getting status reports. Is that what you're saying?"

Low Ability + High Desire -> training and frequent feedback

Medium Ability + High Desire -> coaching with less frequent feedback, often self-assessment

High Ability + High Desire -> empowerment; agree on results and timelines; employee asks for help when needed

PARTICIPATE

"At a very high level – that's most of it," I acknowledged "at least when things are progressing well. The challenge is making sure you match your kind of participation to where the employee is in the situation. For example, if someone is still learning the job but is managed by empowerment, it's like being thrown in the deep end of the pool to learn how to swim. Or, if someone really knows what to do and how to do it, but the manager keeps a close watch – sometimes called micromanaging – then the employee may feel not trusted, patronized, and discounted – all of which could lead to a decreased desire to do the job – or at least to work for that manager."

"I've experienced both of those! It's not fun. But I'd rather be thrown in the deep end than micromanaged."

"It's different for different people. I have always experienced you as someone very willing to take instruction and constructive feedback, but if thrown in the deep end, you'll figure out how to swim."

"Thanks, Dad," she responded. "So, back to my question – how frequently should I meet with an employee? I gather that it depends on the employee and their level of ability and desire related to the tasks they're working on. I like the traffic light approach and can use that whenever we do talk about how things are going. Now I'm wondering if I should wait til they ask, check in randomly, or if we should have a regularly scheduled meeting."

"What're your thoughts?"

"Part of it is their need or desire to know how they're doing, and part of it is my need or desire to know what's going on. I think I should have a meeting with each person at least once a month to at least check in. With some it may be more often or longer, but I need to talk to everyone with a focus on performance and results no less than one time a month," Ariel determined.

"And is there anything else on this one-to-one agenda?" I asked.

"Sure – anything else they want to talk about that we didn't connect on between meetings. Some of them seek me out whenever they need to – which is great. Others tend to wait until there's a significant problem which could be months in between. So, this regularly scheduled meeting should serve as a check in whether it's about their SMART goals progress, work relationships, career direction, or life in general. It will be good to continue to build our relationships more deliberately."

"Sounds like you've got a plan. Many of the people I coach come up with a similar plan but have difficulty sticking with it. Why do you think that might be?"

"I'm guessing other priorities push those meetings aside. Client calls. Boss calls. Budget planning. Various crises. I can imagine there are lots of things that can come up."

"And if the manager cancels the meeting – or the employee does – what's the message?"

"That the meetings are not that important," she commented. "But I think these meetings are critical – almost sacred if the intent is also to continue building the relationship and not just about a status update. I think it's better to have them as scheduled, even if the time is shortened. I want to send the message that our time together is a high priority and that the other person is important to me."

"Great intentions! It will be hard, but keep at it," I suggested. "When we started this conversation, you were wondering how to respond when Sue asks how she is doing. We hit the ground running with the assumption that the question was straightforward and provided objective ways to have the discussion of progress on SMART goals. Would that do it for Sue?"

"Not always. Sometimes I think it's more about how she's feeling about herself or wondering how I or others are feeling about her. It's not really about her work product – it's about her fit with the culture, in relation to others, or that what she's doing matters. That kind of stuff."

"So, how do you think the process we've talked about will help with those kinds of concerns? "

"I believe the one-to-ones with her – especially the other parts of the agenda beyond SMART goals, will provide an opportunity. I also think periodic team building will help build and reinforce the collaborative culture and inter-relationships. And, as you've said to me before, I have a pretty good radar for picking up on things if there's a different reason behind the question."

"Ariel, you do have a great radar for that. Sometimes it can be difficult for the radar operator to notice the blips because of all the other things going on in the environment. But you know, that kind of stuff is often there. So...?

"So every once in a while, whether I suspect something or not, I should just, as you would say, invite the other person to share anything else about how they are feeling about themselves, the team, the work, and so on. And to do it with a tone of voice that doesn't presuppose that there's an issue.... How's that?"

"Sounds good. It ties back to the on-going tasks of motivation and communication. Don't hesitate to consider the bigger picture of the human being – beyond the employee."

"Got it. That's a good reminder."

"Another suggestion, Ariel. You should make some notes about some of the various conversations you have with Sue and others, especially regarding her performance. With so much going on and over time, it's likely you'll forget – or may mis-remember – some conversations. Keeping a record will help you recall positive outcomes, corrective feedback, and progress made over time."

"I've been doing that already. I've been keeping notes like that on various things since I was in middle school and figured out the final exam would cover material from the entire year, not just what we learned in the last couple months. I realized the value of keeping – and reviewing – my notes. As a manager, I have a folder – electronic and hard copy – for each employee and on my own conversations with my boss."

What Does It Mean To Be A Manager?

"Terrific. I should say I'm not surprised," I acknowledged.

"Yeah, it's amazing sometimes how school actually prepared me for life" she chuckled." Then, "Dad, I'm remembering you talked about the bowling analogy. As we're talking, I think it's also important that everyone on the team knows how others are doing – and possibly provide help for team success. What should I do about that?"

"And your thoughts ...?"

"I knew you'd ask me," laughed Ariel. "I think a regularly scheduled team meeting – perhaps every quarter or six months would be a good way to keep us all on the same page. And, before you ask, I think the agenda should include a collective status update using everyone's traffic light for quick reporting. Anyone who has a yellow, or especially a red light, on a SMART goal, should have a chance to throw it out to the team to get any suggestions on how to get to green." She continued, "And I think we should have some kind of team building exercise each time that helps build on the relationships. How does that sound?"

"Fantastic! Awesome! At some point, maybe we'll brainstorm some ideas about team building exercises that can be really powerful for your team. But, I have to jump on a conference call in a few minutes, so I hope this was good enough for now."

"It was. Thanks. Now I have a lot more ideas about how to participate with my employees. Bye."

Chapter 10: PARTICIPATE - Part 2

It was just a few hours later that I called Ariel and left a message. "Hi Ariel. I was thinking about what we talked about earlier today with respect to the management task of participate. I realized we left something out that may be useful. Call me if you're interested and have a few minutes."

Just five minutes later my phone rang. "Hi Dad. Sorry I missed your call. I was just getting some hot cinnamon tea. It's yummy!" I love how she enjoys the small things in life. "I have about 15 minutes before my next meeting. What were you thinking about?"

"I remembered another great model for managing performance that I first learned about in the late 80's."

"Was that the 1880's or just last century?" she teased. She and her siblings we're always suggesting I grew up with dinosaurs running around the neighborhood.

"I choose to ignore that question. Anyway, I think it's another great Ken Blanchard model known as the ABCs of Performance Management."

"Sounds pretty basic. Let's hear it."

"Ok. Like many of these models, I've tweaked it a bit over the years so it's not exactly like the original – but close enough. The 'B' stands for 'Behavior'. Think of this as the decisions and actions someone takes. The 'A' stands for 'Antecedents' or what Blanchard called 'Activators'. In my way of thinking, this is anything the manager does – or doesn't do – that precedes the employee's behavior. But it also includes other things in the environment encouraging or discouraging the behavior. We'll come back to that. And the 'C' stands for 'consequences'. "Consequence' is often thought of as a negative or punishing results. In this model, we'll consider anything that happens as a result of the behavior as a consequence. Does this make sense?"

"So far. Like I joked, it seems pretty basic. I'm guessing there's more to it."

"It's not rocket science, but I think you'll get some value from thinking it through a bit. Earlier, you mentioned that Sue was doing well with respect to the quality of her work, especially the details and deadlines. You also mentioned there are times when she didn't engage with her colleagues as much as you'd like to support collaboration and ensure no one got blind-sided. So, these observable actions constitute her behavior."

"The 'B'. So, you're probably about to ask me what were some of the antecedents, right?"

"Of course!"

"Let's see. The antecedents would probably include her list of goals, the specifics of the project she was working on, her previous experience and the training she's received here."

"Good. What else?"

"Hmm. I may need some help on this," she thought aloud. "You said antecedents can include anything else in the environment that encourages or discourages the behavior.

So, since I had given her positive feedback about her attention to details and meeting deadlines, that probably encouraged her to keep doing those things. And, on the other side, I had mentioned to her a couple times that I wanted her to be more collaborative, but that didn't seem to be positively affecting her current behavior."

"Keep going..." I encouraged, finding it a bit hard not to just jump in with my list.

"Well, I guess she was also watching her colleagues – including me – to get a sense of the norms around here. And to be honest, we're not always as collaborative as I would like us to be – me included. So she may have got an unintentional mixed message."

"Very good. What else?"

"As I think about it, there could be an infinite list! How she was raised at home, what happened in school, our policies and procedures, time pressures, the physical environment and tools that help or hinder collaboration. The list can go on and on – much of which is ancient history or out of my control."

"You're right. It's important to recognize how much stuff

influences a person's behavior in any given moment – and to recognize there are a lot of factors you can't do anything about. The value of thinking about this, is that there are a lot of antecedents that you *can* do something about to help set her up for success – that is, that her behavior is what you desire."

"OK – that helps. If I want Sue – or anyone else for that matter – to do something in the way I desire, I have to try to ensure that the antecedents are in place that will support her behaving in that way," Ariel summarized. "What about the 'C' – consequences? You suggested we be careful not to think of them as just negatives or punishing."

"There are two parts to consequences I want to briefly explore with you. First, let's hear some of your ideas about what kinds of consequences there could be in general – that is categories of rewards or punishments."

"If I'm understanding you correctly, those categories of consequences could include some kind of feedback, some kind of performance recognition, perhaps some compensation adjustment, different opportunities on the job, levels of engagement with colleagues. That kind of stuff. Was that what you mean?" she asked.

"Exactly. Those and more – probably another exhaustive list. Now, think of each of those categories as objectively as possible – no load as to whether they are good or bad. The perception of their value and subsequent impact will be in how they are perceived by Sue and how her perception of any consequence serves as an antecedent to further behavior."

"So – there is always a consequence from any behavior. How that consequence is perceived – no matter how I may have intended it – will effect whatever she does next. I learned something about this in my psych classes and it's coming back to me now."

"Good – then let's go to the second point about consequences – focusing on how they are perceived and lead to further action."

"OK – I'm remembering that consequences can be perceived as positive, or negative, somewhere in between, or mixed. Is that right?"

"Yes. We're not going to go into all the interesting brain research that helps to examine these things much deeper. For our purposes – we'll focus on the management task of participate to help Sue in the sustaining phase of her career

What Does It Mean To Be A Manager?

– we'll keep to a fairly high level."

"Good, 'cause I'm going to start running out of time pretty soon and I have some antecedents to go over before my next meeting or there may be some undesirable consequences."

"Alright," I chuckled. "So if a person does a behavior and experiences what she perceives as a positive consequence, what's the likely next behavior?"

"This is simple positive reinforcement," Ariel declared. "She'll likely repeat that performance next time."

"And it may also encourage her to go beyond the previous performance because she's developed confidence and had a positive feeling she wants to experience again," I added.

"Yes, I remember that, too. After awhile, the same level of positive reinforcement can lose some of it's power. We heard some story about how they design casinos. Near the entrances are slot machines that pay out frequently, but only a little each time. Players seeking more reward move toward the interior where the more expensive machines pay out less frequently but at higher amounts. And eventually, the casino can attract some players to some very expensive games where they most often lose, but when they win, there's a huge payoff. I remember that was called 'intermittent reinforcement'. Mom always warned us not to laugh at your puns even infrequently, because the intermittent reinforcement was the strongest kind to encourage you to do more."

"OK – you understand the concept and I'll ignore the jab." I snickered. "Now, let's look at what might be experienced as a negative consequence – even if that was not what was intended. How might a negative consequence be an antecedent to the next behavior?"

"Well, it would depend on the severity of the consequence. I think most of the time, a negative consequence makes it less likely that the person will do the undesired behavior again. Yet, I'm thinking about a number of people I know who keep on doing something despite what I would think of as negative consequences. Maybe the punishment isn't strong enough," suggested Ariel.

"Could be. Or it could be that the reward of changing is not strong enough, either. Way back when I was a schoolteacher, I remember having some students who would act out. In many cases I realized they felt starved for attention and acting out, even with the negative consequences, was a way to get attention – which was a positive reward for them. I had to find ways to give them appropriate attention *and* have them change their inappropriate behaviors. It worked sometimes, but it is hard to change a lifetime of behavior patterns in just a few hours per day, especially if the old behaviors are reinforced elsewhere. Like we said earlier, you and I don't control all the antecedents."

"I can see where this can be a bit more complicated. Sue – and all the rest of us - brings all the rest of her life with her to the job."

"That's why we talked about motivation early on. Whether managers want to or not, they have to deal with the whole person."

"I actually really like that about the job," Ariel declared.

"Me, too. So – one more point: Consequences that are perceived as neutral or non-existent. What's the likely next behavior?"

"Well, let me think about that a moment," she paused. "Thinking back over my own experiences and what I saw with others, there are a number of possibilities. First, the perceived lack of a consequence could lead to someone just doing more of the same behavior at the same level. Or, they might turn it up a notch to gain more attention." She thought some more. "I know people who have such positive self-esteem – deservedly or not - that no consequence seems to matter that much. They just 'know' they're good. And I know people with a lower self-esteem who would assume they'd messed up if they don't hear anything positive."

"So, again, what's the next likely behavior?" I repeated.

"It's hard to predict. It seems that it could go a number of different ways – doing more of the same; kicking it up a notch; or stopping the behavior. My guess, is over time, most people who want consequences in the way of feedback, will eventually stop doing the behavior if they feel like it doesn't seem to matter to anyone."

"So, as an oversimplification, sometimes the lack of feedback, or receiving what is perceived as neutral consequences, can produce the same kind of results as negative consequences – that is, the person stops doing the behavior because it doesn't seem to matter."

"I'm still not sure about that, Dad. I think each situation and person may be different."

"Good point. Here's what I think is important to consider. I know a lot of managers who seem to believe that as long as people are doing the desired behaviors, that the employee thinks no news is good news. That is, they tell me, 'The employee *knows* she's doing OK if I don't point out a problem.' Actually, the 'problem' may arise that the employee, not knowing they are doing things right, may change or stop the behavior trying to get some kind of feedback or consequence."

Ariel jumped in - "This reminds me of the bowling example you told me before. If I don't know what actually happened behind the curtain, I may either keep trying different things or stop bowling altogether, when, in fact, I may have been knocking down most of the pins. I know that I want to know how I did and that someone else noticed as well."

"OK. I think you've got it. As your coach, I'll ask you to summarize what you've learned so far about the ABCs of performance management."

"Sure. As a manager, I have some idea of the behaviors I want my employee to demonstrate. Those behaviors have many antecedents that determine if and how she will perform. I have influence on some antecedents – such as the work environment, clarity of desired outcomes, training, and so on that will support her doing what I want. There are other antecedents over which I have less or no influence, such as the skills, knowledge, and experiences she brings from her previous work or her whole life." After a short pause, "And every behavior has a consequence. It can be perceived by her to be a positive consequence, which encourages her to repeat the behavior or do even more. Or she could perceive a negative consequence, which would usually cause her to do less of that behavior or stop it all together. However, sometimes, it could cause her to do even more if she was just looking for attention. And, if she perceives no consequence or just a neutral response, she may take it in the same way as a negative consequence and either repeat the same behavior, kick it up a bit, or stop it altogether. Whew!! That's a lot of pop psychology!"

Perceived as	Next likely behavior
Positive	- Repeat same
	- Do even more of same
Negative	- Stop
	- Do even more of same for reward of attention
Neutral or non-existent	- Continue same
	- Do more of same for reward of attention
	- Stop

What Does It Mean To Be A Manager?

"Well done! You seem to have a good grasp on the ABC's as we've discussed them so far. Are you up for one further piece about consequences?"

"Let's do it!" Ariel said enthusiastically. I could tell she was pleased with herself for being able to articulate what we'd explored so far.

"So, there are four characteristics of consequences that can influence a person's choice about their next actions. Whether they perceive the consequence as positive or negative – and remember that neutral or no consequence is often perceived as negative – these four characteristics are a strong influence on what happens next, especially where a choice is involved."

"What do you mean 'where a choice is involved'?"

"Some actions create consequences and further actions automatically – like touching a hot burner on the stove and quickly pulling back your hand. Other actions are not so automatic. For example, driving over the speed limit on the expressway. There is a choice that the driver makes every moment to continue or stop that behavior. That choice depends on these four characteristics."

PARTICIPATE - Part 2

"Ok, now you've got my attention," Ariel responded. "I often wondered about the way you drive, especially when Mom is telling you to slow down."

"Humph!" I laughed. "So, when I am aware of my driving behavior and that there is choice involved, I first consider what the risks are of going over the speed limit."

"Well," interrupted Ariel, "Mom's making a comment would be one. Also, getting a ticket or having an accident are more likely. Also, you're probably not getting as good gas mileage."

"Correct. Are there any possible positive consequences?"

"Sure. You could get where you're going faster. And, I guess, if everyone else is speeding, it may actually be safer to drive faster."

"If we took time to think about it, we could probably list further potential positive or negative consequences to my behavior. But for now, let me tell you a true story that will help to illustrate this," I suggested. "Back when your older sister was finishing her freshman year at college, I drove out to pick her up, planning to arrive at 6 pm. I was a little behind schedule, so as I drove across Iowa, I set my cruise control at 14 miles over the posted limit. I assumed the police would probably allow 15 over without stopping me based on previous experience. So, I thought the *certainty* of a ticket was a minimal risk. Further, I had been driving over the speed limit for some time, so the *immediacy* of a negative consequence seemed low risk as well. Also, I often drive over the limit and have only been stopped a very few times over the years and had not paid much in fines. So the *frequency* as well as the *strength* of negative consequences both seemed acceptable risks when balanced against my desire to arrive as planned. I was cruising along when all of a sudden there were flashing lights in the rearview mirror and I pulled off on the shoulder."

"Oh my!" Ariel exclaimed.

"Well, the officer came up and asked me where I was going and if I knew how fast I was driving. I honestly told him about my scheduled arrival time and how fast I was driving according to my cruise control. Then he did all the license and registration stuff and went to his patrol car to check if I had any priors or other offenses. When he returned to my open driver's window, he said all that was OK and he wasn't going to give me a ticket. But then he asked if I had seen him on the other side of the highway as I sped by. I hadn't. I had been running on cruise control listening to the radio and scanning the environment where very little traffic was to be seen. He then said, 'Here's the problem with that. In this section of the highway, the woods come fairly close to the expressway. We've had a lot of deer running out of the woods right onto the road and had a number of serious accidents, including some fatalities. Now, I know you want to get to your daughter quickly, but you have to drive more safely if you want to get to her at all.'" I took a breath and continued. "So I had chosen a behavior, speeding, analyzing the potential certainty, immediacy, frequency and strength of the consequence of getting a ticket. What he said about a more powerful potential consequence is what really changed my behavior. It was now OK if I arrived a bit late."

"Interesting story, Dad. I'm glad you made it there safely. And, I understand that when my employee is engaging in a behavior I either want to reinforce or change, I have to help her consider how she's making her choices, and possibly help her understand a more significant consequence than what she may have been considering. For the situation we talked about with Sue, the more significant consequence is that the lack of collaboration will make future projects that much harder and possibly jeopardize our overall results and ability to serve our clients."

What Does It Mean To Be A Manager?

"Ariel, I think you got this nailed. One last question: Now that you understand how antecedents lead to certain behaviors and how consequences can reinforce or change those behaviors, which do you think is more useful for a manager in the participate tasks?"

"I want to say 'both' and 'it depends'. But I know you'll ask me again. So, I'm going with 'antecedents'. In the work that I do, a lot of it focuses on specifics of consequences of people's actions. I have always felt if we can work on the causes of inappropriate behaviors, we have a better chance of changing the systemic problems. And, before you ask, what that means for me as a manager is that I have to do whatever I can to set people up for success rather than trying to correct potential mistakes. This all makes a lot of sense to me. Thanks for reminding me of the ABCs, Dad."

"Glad it seems helpful. Your insights will be useful not only in the sustaining phase, but throughout all employee performance phases."

"Thanks again. I'm heading off to another meeting in a few minutes and I have some antecedents to prepare. Love you. Drive safely."

PARTICIPATE - Part 3

Chapter 11: PARTICIPATE – Part 3

"Dad," she said, after I picked up my office phone. "I have some more questions for you. Do you have a few minutes?"

I looked at my computer screen where several open documents were calling out to me to complete the agenda planning for an upcoming strategic planning retreat. Nothing I couldn't get back to in a few minutes. "Just a moment. Let me save the documents I was working on." After a few clicks, "OK, whatcha got?"

What Does It Mean To Be A Manager?

"Well, I realize a lot of what we've been talking about on employee performance phases and the accompanying management tasks is really helpful when I'm working one on one with an employee. Next week, we're doing an off-site with the team and I was wondering how the participate task relates."

"Great question, and I know you've had a lot of experience participating in and leading team building. So, let's see if our conversation can help you remember what you already know as well as perhaps offer a few other ideas."

"OK. First, I have to start with the three P's we've talked about – purpose, process, and payoff. With input from others, I've pretty much firmed up two purposes – one is to get to know each other better personally and the other is to understand each other's roles and how we can best meet our goals. I haven't finalized a process yet, but my payoff – what I hope for – is that when we leave the off-site, everyone will have a deeper understanding of themselves and the people we collaborate with and some specific ideas on how to be even more collectively productive. The real measure of success will show up over the following weeks with all projects getting completed on time, with higher quality, and a positive energy that together we're making a difference."

"Sounds like a great start. You've painted a picture of a future state that is very attractive. To what extent have you shared all this with the team and what's been the response?"

"Everyone has had some input and each person is very excited. Some are offering to help plan or lead different parts of what we do."

"Terrific! So, this is primarily working with a good team and helping them be even better versus some interpersonal or work issues, right?"

"I think so. I am not aware of any conflicts – or differences – that need to be addressed at this time. I know there are some different personalities, and different ideas on how to approach the work, but there's nothing that has or is about to blow up."

"Good. Then, let's focus on some things you can do together that will focus on strengths and build further positive momentum. If you ever have some interpersonal conflicts, you know you can call me to discuss those as well," I offered. "So, for now, given the first purpose of helping people know each other better, what kinds of things are you thinking of? What worked well for you before?"

What Does It Mean To Be A Manager?

"One thing I was thinking of was something I did in an orientation program. At first I thought it might be rather cliché, but it really gave me some insights into myself and others. The activity was called 'two truths and a lie'. As we went around the group, each person was to say three things about themselves that others didn't already know. We had to tell a brief story about each one. Two of those stories were to be true, and one was fictional. Then others had to identify which one they thought was made up. It was interesting to learn about each other's truths, and fascinating to try and figure out which story was made up."

"I really like that exercise. What did you learn from participating?"

"Some of my friends were in the group – people I thought I knew pretty well. I was amazed at some of the things about which I had no idea! And, hearing those things kind of gave me new insights into each person and put some other stuff in a broader context. Also, it became more engaging as people really worked to tell their made-up experience in a convincing way to try and fool the rest of us. There were some really bazaar stories – some of which were actually the truths!"

"What else did you learn?"

"No real surprise – but I had trouble lying. Some people were really creative and I couldn't tell from their story or body language what was fact or fiction. Some people really made up some whoppers and some people just tweaked the truth a little bit. I tried to tell a whopper, but I guess my body language must have given me away because most everyone figured out which two stories I told were true and which one was the lie. I guess I just have to be truthful all the time, because people can easily tell when I'm not."

"So, if you do that activity, how do you believe it will help achieve your purpose?"

"Well, it will be fun! We'll also get to know who can be creative in this context and fool the rest of us, but that it's important to be truthful if we really want to achieve great things together."

"OK. Not every activity has to be profound. You want the variety of things you do to all work together to help achieve the results. This one helps you to learn different facts about each other and to get some sense of individual creativity and the ability to discern fact from fiction. What else are you thinking about doing?"

What Does It Mean To Be A Manager?

"I've done a couple personality assessments over the years. I thought having everyone do one of those would help each of us know ourselves better and would be a way to understand how to work with the different styles in the team."

"There are many good ones that can help in that regard. I'm trained in six of them myself. I just caution you to remember, despite claims of validity and reliability, in my opinion no personality assessment is an absolute. No matter which one you choose to use, in the debriefing and follow up, you should rely on it not as a landing pad, but as a launching pad to further insight. Be careful not to put yourself or others in a personality box. There are so many variables that can have a person show up differently in a given situation. However, these tools can be great for gaining insight, seeing trends, and learning ways to adapt to be more effective in different situations with different people."

"Well, I'm looking at a few different ones that focus on preferences or actual behaviors. I may come back to you to get further ideas."

"OK – what else are you considering for the off-site?"

"I remember something about a window through which to see yourself and others. I can't quite recall the name, but I remember something about 'blind spots.' Do you know what I'm talking about?"

"It sounds like the Johari Window," I suggested.

"That's it! I remember the name because it was named after the two guys who came up with it – Joe and Harry. Right?"

"Yes. Actually Joseph Luft and Harrington Ingham. It's a great tool for helping build a team's openness and authenticity. That's right in line with your payoff of effective collaboration."

"My memory is a bit weak on this one. Can you walk me through it?" Ariel requested.

"Sure. And you can find numerous materials on it with an internet search as well. And also, like so many other tools, I've adjusted it a bit as I've become more familiar with it over the years," I clarified. "Like so many other management tools, it starts out like a 4-quadrant model. The upper-left box is what I know about myself *and* what others know about me. This is my 'public domain' or 'arena'. Below that in the lower left is what I know about myself and have not shared with others. This is my 'private domain' or what some call my 'façade'. The upper-right box is what you were remembering as my 'blind spots'. These are things that other people perceive about me and that I am unaware of myself. The bottom-right box is things not known to me and also not known to others. It is referred to as the 'unknown', but I often think of it as 'unaware'. Then I put another box below that as a kind of shadow. These are things that are possibly unknowable without some deeper assistance such as from therapy. It's not simply an act of becoming aware."

"I think I got it."

Public Domain (Arena)	Blind Spots
Private Domain (Facade)	Unknown (Unaware)

Unknowable

"Great. Now let's talk about how the Johari Window can help build relationships in your team. The size of the arena you have with any other person or people is one indication of the quality or depth of your relationship. That is, the larger the arena for each of you, the deeper or stronger the relationships can be. So the question regarding your off-site might be how to enlarge each person's arena."

"Keep going," Ariel encouraged.

"There are a few ways to increase the size of the public domain. Some may come from your initiative, some from another person's. Since you're creating a picture, let's start with you drawing an arrow from your private domain up into your public domain. Label that 'tell'. This represents you intentionally sharing something about yourself that the other person doesn't know. We talked about that in the first exercise of two truths and a lie. "

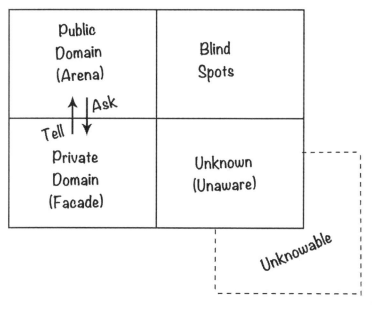

"That works if the other person knows which things are true and which aren't," Ariel clarified. "And, I guess I'm revealing something about myself also just in the way I tell the stories."

"Exactly. We are revealing things about ourselves intentionally or otherwise all the time. We can consider those things that we both are aware of now as part of the arena. We'll come back to blind spots in a few moments." I paused. "Now, draw an arrow from the arena pointing into the private domain and label it 'ask'. This represents when the other person asks you to reveal more of yourself. Depending on your openness, you might answer their questions. If you feel the questions are too close to home, that the person is being nosy, or whatever, you can choose not to share as deeply."

"Yeah," responded Ariel. "As open as I like to think I am, there are some things that I don't want to share unless I have a deep connection with that person first. I guess we all have our boundaries."

"That's right. And it's within your control – usually – if and what to share from your private domain and how much that might change as the relationship evolves. Now, let's go another direction. Draw an arrow from your blind spots to your arena and label that 'tell'. This is what happens when someone tells you something about yourself that they are aware of and you were not. This is another form of feedback and often quite revealing."

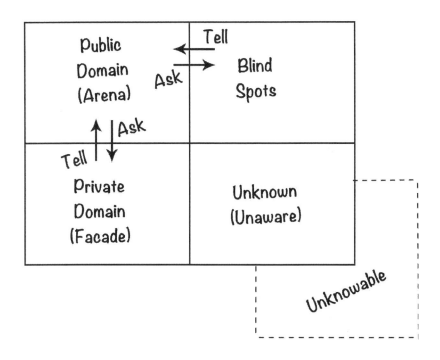

"Sorry to jump in again. I can name several people who do this with me or others. They just seem to have a need to give their opinion of what they believe I am thinking or doing. It can be annoying at times, especially if I don't think they are right."

"OK. A couple things. Sure, some people just jump at the

chance to tell you what they think of you. Two things to consider – their intention may be to share something from your blind spots. That perception is actually coming from *their* private domain and may be an effort to enlarge your arena with them – to build the relationship. Remember my rule – 99.9% of people 99.9% of the time mean well. Also, their perception is just that – not true or false. Remember the ladder of inference. That person has experienced the reality of you and immediately filtered that through her own experience, assumptions, conclusions and beliefs. If you choose, you can share your ladders of inference and again have an opportunity to build on the relationship."

"OK. And the second thing?"

"Remember our conversation about trust? You said at a basic level, you trust someone if they are honest with you – that they tell you the truth. Sharing their truth with you this way provides an opportunity to go beyond being just honest – to be candid. Their candor is intended to help you become aware of something you may not have known."

Ariel said, "Got it. And to continue, I guess there's an arrow from my arena to my blind spot labeled 'ask'. That would be me inviting the other person to share their perceptions of me that I may not have been aware of."

"Absolutely. And again, you have some control over what and how much you ask and how you take in what the other person shares."

"This is useful," Ariel responded. "Are there arrows to or from the unknown box?"

"Think it through. What are your ideas?"

"Well, I think if something is known in the arena, private domain, or blind spots, it can't be pushed into the unknown. On the other hand, if something was unknown about me and neither of us was aware of it until this moment, it could be moved to either my private domain or my blind spot and from there possibly into my arena." Ariel paused. "I'm having trouble thinking of an example of this, though."

"OK. Try this. When you went to work today, did anything happen that you hadn't expected – and also seemed to catch someone else by surprise?"

"Sure. We had a client come in and start to complain about some services she felt she was entitled to but not receiving. She was blaming Sue for intentionally withholding some benefits. Initially I had no idea what was going on and Sue seemed baffled as well."

What Does It Mean To Be A Manager?

"So, at that moment, the information and situation were unknowns. What did you and Sue do?"

"We asked her to calmly tell us more specifics. It turned out that the client was mistaken - that the benefits would be forthcoming after six weeks, not four. We got things worked out and checked for clarity and understanding. That was fairly minor, but that kind of thing happens a lot."

"It sounds like you and Sue used your communication skills, the ladder of inference, and so on to get the situation taken care of. Now, let me ask you this – during this experience did you have some perceptions about Sue and how she was handling the situation? And do you think she had some perceptions of you as well?"

"Of course."

"Those thoughts and feelings you each had were in the unknown box until the experience happened. Now that each of you has some awareness, you could intentionally choose to share some of your perceptions with one another. In part, this would be further on-the-job coaching, but it is also about continually strengthening the relationship. Of course, it's not necessary to do this kind of sharing each time anything happens. On the other hand, if you have a strong feeling or thought, it's probably useful to put it out there."

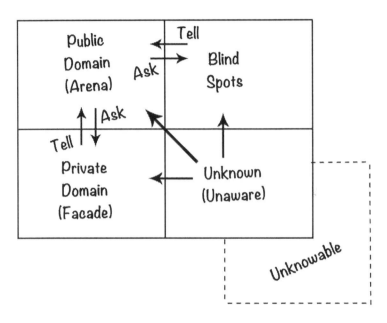

"Thanks. That clarifies it a bit. So, I have my picture of the Johari Window with the arrows in various directions. Now, I have to decide if and how to use it in the team's off-site."

"Let's go back to where you started about the purpose and payoff you have targeted. If I heard you correctly, you want all the team members to know more about themselves and others so that they can collaborate even more effectively. Right?"

"Right."

What Does It Mean To Be A Manager?

"So if we consider the Johari Window, you've had people learning more about themselves through the personal style assessment and the sharing of two truths and a lie. What's missing?"

"Hearing from each other about our blind spots!" declared Ariel.

"OK. What might you do to hear from each other about your blind spots?"

"I would think it would work best if I go first and invite others to share their perceptions of me that may be in my blind spots," Ariel suggested. "I wonder how much people would share, whether it would be positive or negative, and how I might respond, even if I disagree."

"Those are great questions, Ariel. Let's go over a few possibilities. First, you might suggest a structure that helps people formulate their thoughts and feelings. One way I use a lot goes like this: 'When you do/say X, I feel/think Y'. For example, 'Ariel, when you ask questions about my suggestions, I sense that you are really interested in what I have to say'. Or, 'Ariel, when you ask questions about my suggestions, sometimes I hear a judgmental tone and I assume you disagree with what I'm saying, or perhaps even think I'm dumb to suggest that idea'."

"Wow, so the same behavior of my asking questions could elicit very different responses. That sounds like it could just confuse things. How do I know what to do about this?"

"A further suggestion to the structure might be to request a second part to the other person's feedback. After 'When you do/say X, I feel/think Y' add 'It would help me if you would Z'. For example, Ariel, when you ask questions about my suggestions, sometimes I hear a judgmental tone and I assume you disagree with what I'm saying, or perhaps even think I'm dumb to suggest that idea. It would help me if you would clarify whether you think my suggestion was useful or not and in what ways'."

"That still seems like I could have a lot of questions about the feedback. I would probably want to know more."

"OK. Then the next thing you could do is request a specific, hopefully recent, example of that behavior. If you make such a request, be aware of your tone of voice and body language. Remember, this person is sharing something from their private domain in order to build their relationship with you. Be open and curious, and try not to become proud or defensive. So – 'Ariel, when you ask questions about my suggestions, sometimes I hear a judgmental tone and I assume you disagree with what I'm saying, or perhaps even think I'm dumb to suggest that idea. It would help me if you would clarify whether you think my suggestion was useful or not and in what ways. For example, earlier in our conversation today, you said, 'Thanks, that clarifies it a bit.' Having heard that the suggestion was useful to you (positive reinforcement) I am more likely to offer others in the hope that they, too, will be useful."

"Dad, I don't want your head to get too big, but most of your suggestions are helpful. And I like that you ask me questions so I have the opportunity to hear my own thoughts, also quite good sometimes, if I do say so myself," she chuckled.

"Moving right along…" I interjected. "The last – and perhaps most challenging part of this process for the one getting feedback, is how to respond once you've heard the perceptions about your possible blind spots. I like to think that when someone is willing to share their feedback, to reveal something from their private domain, it is to improve or deepen the relationship. That's a real gift. And, in polite society, when someone gives you a gift, what is the appropriate thing to say?"

"Thank you."

"Exactly and entirely!" I exclaimed. "Once you have understood what the other person said, whether you agree or not, simply and sincerely say, 'Thank you'. Make it easy for them to give you the gift. Don't deny that you deserve it – such as 'it wasn't just me'. Don't make light of it – such as 'just doing my job'. Or any other potential discount. Simply and sincerely say, 'Thank you'."

"That's more good advice, and I like the way you point out how simply and sincerely saying 'Thank you' makes it easier on the other person to give feedback."

"Thank you," I replied. "Many times when I have led this with teams, it has been very powerful and emotional. You might consider having a skilled facilitator who can help with the depth and pacing. He or she may only have to remind the listener to simply say 'thank you'."

"OK. Let me think about that for this exercise and some of the other things we've discussed, including a further exploration of our cultural values. A lot of what we've talked about is focused on the human side of our collaborating, which I think is the most important. However, we also have the work side to consider – who does what and how do we help each other get the desired results," Ariel acknowledged. "What suggestions do you have about that?" Then quickly, "Wait a moment, I know you're going to ask me what ideas I have. So, I want to review the overall team goals and why they are important. Then I think I'll ask each person to share what their role is in helping achieve those goals."

"Sounds good. Here are a couple additional possibilities you might consider. First, jointly create a diagram for some of the major processes your team does. For example, you might start with a client interaction. When she comes in the door, who does what first? Then what happens and who does it? And so on to see the process flow through the team leading to the final result. Another example might be how the team generates a report to upper management, the board, or investors and funders."

"I think just identifying a number of those processes will be helpful. So after we create the process flow diagram, what's next?"

"A second action might be to improve the processes. Every organization has external customers it serves. And every organization has external suppliers from whom it gets raw materials, information and so on. This is also true inside the organization. So when you look at your diagram, identify who are internal suppliers and who are internal customers at any transition point – or handoff – in the process. Then, put together suppliers with customers for each transition so they can talk about what is working well and what could be improved. For example, if the internal supplier is providing information to the internal customer, does the customer feel she is getting all the necessary, relevant and sufficient information she needs? Is it delivered in the way she wants it – written, email, phone, spreadsheet. Does it contain the appropriate level of detail and clarification for next steps? And is it delivered when she wants it – not too soon and not too late? And so on."

"So by clarifying what the customer wants, how and when, the supplier has a better chance of providing those things. And, I can see there could be a whole lot of those conversations throughout the process so everyone not only knows their role, but can adjust it to make it work even better for their internal customer. That makes a lot of sense."

"Ariel, it sounds easier than it may be. There are so many handoffs in so many processes, it can take a while to get through everything. When you and the team start to identify some of these processes, start with what seem to be the easier ones to get some practice. Or, try to identify the ones with obvious shortcomings – the low-hanging fruit – that can be more easily improved. Then you can build on the momentum."

"More things for me to think about. Thanks Dad," she said with a humorous sigh.

"Yes, there's a lot here, and you don't have to do everything all at once. And, as you are starting to think about all this and what you might do at the off-site, is there anything you think could make it difficult to accomplish what you want? Any concerns?"

"A few – most having to do with time and trying to bite off more than we can chew. Yet, as I think of all that we've talked about already, I guess I still want some way to reinforce the feeling that we're all in this together and that what we do really matters."

"Sounds like a great opportunity to revisit the motivation task. You'll recall that motivation runs throughout all performance phases. Your task is to help an employee feel the connection between what she values and wants in her life and how doing what and how you want on the job can help her get what she wants. The same can be said when working with a team. Now, this may sound a bit woo-woo. I believe work can be a spiritual experience. Not in a religious sense, but in the following way. A spiritual experience is one in which I feel connected to something greater than myself and that through that connection I contribute something that matters – that makes a positive difference. Further, that I may make that contribution in relationship with other people with whom I have mutual care and respect. And, that we periodically celebrate our efforts and remember together our connection to a purpose greater than ourselves."

"You're right. It does sound a bit woo-woo, but not in a kumbaya kind of way. If I get your meaning, I have to help us all remember our collective greater purpose and our contribution to making a better world. Everyone on my team wants to make a difference, and we need to remind ourselves of that purpose and celebrate our efforts. It's not just improving work processes, it's about serving clients and working to improve the antecedents in the world leading to better behaviors and positive consequences," Ariel passionately declared.

"At your off-site, and any other time you can, use that passion to re-enforce the connection to the greater purpose. It really works," I encouraged.

"Thanks, Dad. I will. That was the missing piece that pulls together the real value of the off-site; in fact, all the work we do. Now I'm going to finish mapping out the agenda and keep in mind the greater purpose and the spiritual nature of what we do together. Thanks for your time and insights once again. I love you."

"I love you, too," I said, the smile coming through in my voice. As I returned to my open documents for the strategic planning retreat agenda I was working on, I thought about how I could help my client get that spiritual sense of the work they were doing as well. I recognized, yet again, how my work gives me that sense of connection - how it feeds my soul - and how much I learn from every conversation.

EVALUATE

Chapter 12: EVALUATE

It had been about 6 weeks since Ariel and I talked in depth about her management practices. We'd had lots of family conversations and caught up in general about how each other's lives were progressing. She had shared briefly that the off-site team building had gone extremely well and everyone really bought into SMART goals and collaboration and how everything they did individually and collectively was serving of a greater purpose. They were using one of their conference rooms as a kind of command center. They had process flow diagrams posted indicating who had what roles and if they had met to clarify and improve the handoff

What Does It Mean To Be A Manager?

processes. Additionally, they had posted their team SMART goals and traffic-light charts for everyone so they could see the progress and offer assistance where possible. Additionally, each person had created a small sign posted at their workstation indicating her personal style preferences and reminders on how best to work collaboratively. Ariel felt proud of herself and her team.

On a Sunday evening, after some catch up over the phone, Ariel reported, "Things are really humming. Sure, we have challenges pop up from time to time. We seem to be able to call a time out and share our ladders of inference about what's going on, leverage our personal styles to help us communicate more effectively, and remembering our greater purpose, most of the time come up with solutions that work well for everyone. "

"It's great to hear how well things are going for everyone. What's next for you?"

"Well, that's one of the reasons I wanted to talk with you. In a couple weeks, we're starting our annual review process. I wanted to get some tips for how to prepare and have the review discussions."

"OK. Sounds like you're moving onto the next task of

management in the sustaining phase of employee performance. That's the task I call 'Evaluate'. You've already been doing a lot of evaluation informally as parts of the educate and participate tasks. Now it sounds like you're moving into the more formal aspects."

"Yep. These performance reviews will be documented and put into each employee's personnel record. They are also used to determine merit pay increases and potential for promotion."

"Does your organization have a defined process and/or forms for you to use?" I asked, knowing that every organization has unique expectations and processes for formal reviews. Sometimes they are called by different names, each with their own connotation. Whether it's a 'review', 'assessment', 'appraisal', or 'evaluation' – it can be the most-anxiety producing part of the manager-employee relationship for either or both the employee and the manager. I wanted to help Ariel understand what her organization uses as well as some general practices to help it be a very productive process.

"We have some forms to fill out and a rating scale. I think I can fill in all the blanks and give a fair rating, but I want it to be more valuable than just that. This is an opportunity to more-deeply engage with each employee in a longer-term perspective and also for motivation as we've talked about it before."

"OK. Here's a list of possible topics for us to work through. Feel free to add to the list or to select which ones you want to discuss. First, there's preparation – pulling together whatever information is necessary, relevant and sufficient for reviewing the past year. Second, is preparing for the conversation, which may include reviewing an employee's self-assessment, completing a draft of your own assessment of their performance, and thinking through how to have the conversation. These next three can be in any order and depend on if, how and when your organization does things. So third you need to determine a rating based on the work done since the last review, complete whatever administrative paperwork, compensation planning, and so on. Fourth, you may also have a discussion about the employee's development plan and career possibilities. And fifth, you may do formal goal setting for the next review period."

"That's a lot – and I want it all!" Ariel stated. "We are not a formal organization when it comes to these kinds of things, but perhaps I can help improve the process, or at least have more-productive conversations with my employees, especially if they've been through this before and it was a bit traumatic. That's happened to me and it was really hard."

"The first general rule,'" I declared, "is - no surprises. If you've done a good job throughout the year participating with the employee, setting and tracking SMART goals, giving positive and corrective feedback, and so on, the formal review should 'simply' be a recalling and documenting of things you've already talked about."

"Yep, and I have all my notes about those conversations. I had also encouraged my employees to keep their own notes knowing that this time would be coming."

"Great. So does it make sense to follow on with that and talk more about how else to prepare?"

"Let's do it!" exclaimed Ariel.

"First of all, again with the idea of no surprises, you should review all the SMART goals and double check that you and your employee were on the same page from the get-go. Further, if there were any changes in goals or expectations during the year, that should also have been communicated and clear to both of you. I can't tell you how many times I've heard about someone saying, 'I didn't know I was supposed to do that!'"

What Does It Mean To Be A Manager?

"I think I'm good there. I've been meeting regularly with each employee to review the status of their goals and special projects."

"Terrific. Most organizations review the results of *what* was to be accomplished. Some go further and look at *how* those results were accomplished."

"What do you mean by 'how'?" Ariel asked.

"Your guess?" I prompted.

"I guess it could include things like how someone engaged with their co-workers, clients, and me. You and I have talked about the importance of collaboration before. So I guess it's not just that the work got done, but how well someone collaborated with others."

"Or on some projects, it could even be the opposite – that the employee was able to work independently to accomplish a task."

"Oh, I see. So it depends on the situation and we needed to be clear up front and throughout the year on the expectations not only of what, but also how," Ariel stated.

EVALUATE

"Right. Now, what might be some other how's that could be a part of what you expected from your employees?"

"Well, again, depending on the person and the situation, I expected sometimes that people would take initiative and try to move things forward, and other times that they should check with me before taking further action. I expected them to use good judgment." She paused. "And, I want them to always act with integrity and do what's best for the client and the organization. And I want them to always be thinking of how to make things better in how we do our work. " She paused again. "And I want them to dress appropriately, show up to meetings on time and prepared, and generally to act professionally. I could keep going on and on."

"As you said, the how can involve many things. Some have to do with the organization's values, some with its culture and norms, and so on. If there are specific how's that you plan to review, you hopefully communicated those up front – and provided training and feedback throughout the process so by review time there would be…"

"No surprises!" Ariel exclaimed.

"One other comment about the how: in some organizations they include how kinds of things in job descriptions, lists of competencies, values statements, and employee handbooks describing cultural norms and expectations. This practice means the manager doesn't necessarily have to discuss it with respect to each task. I think it is still useful to have periodic reminders as positive reinforcement, corrective feedback, or when something a bit out of the ordinary is requested."

"OK – so my preparation should double check the what and how of the work and my notes from various conversations we had throughout the year. Anything else?"

"Again, depending on the situation, you might also solicit feedback from third parties including co-workers, clients – internal and external, and anyone else who may have had interaction with your employee relative to her work."

"Interesting. How would I do that?" she asked. "Oops. I know you'll turn that around. So, I guess I could talk to them and ask for their input. Or, I could conduct a brief written survey."

"And what specific input are you looking for?"

"I want to hear their opinions – no, make that facts – about my employee. So, whatever they say, I may have to probe a

---

bit deeper to get evidence, real stories of what and how my employee worked with them."

"Good. And you might also ask the third party to identify any particular strengths or areas for improvement they experienced," I added.

"Should that input be confidential?"

I waited, and after a moment of silence, she said, "It depends. Sometimes I'd want to be able to refer to things I'd heard with specific examples. So what I hear can't be confidential. Other times, I'd be listening for trends and combining a variety of input. I should probably be clear upfront with any third party of how I want to use their input and get permission to refer to any specifics. Or, if that person is uncomfortable being named or quoted, I have to honor that request."

"A lot of that will depend on the culture and values of the organization. If you want more transparency across the board, these kinds of third party comments should already have been shared with your employee at the time of the interactions, so by the review time, there should be ... "

"No surprises! Got it. I don't think our culture is there yet, so

What Does It Mean To Be A Manager?

I'll have to be thoughtful about who I solicit input from and check the desire for confidentiality. As I think about it, I believe there will be more than enough corroborating evidence for anything we'll talk about in the review."

"Great. So, in general, you've got all your data from various sources. Your next action is to put these in whatever format or form used in your organization. Having things written down in that common format helps with consistency across all your employees and across the entire organization."

"Dad, you mentioned something earlier that I want to go back to before we move on. You said something about the employee doing a self-assessment."

"That's right. In some organizations, there is a requirement that each employee completes a self-assessment. Sometimes that is given to the manager prior to the review meeting; sometimes it is brought to the meeting without the manager seeing it first. For that matter, the same is sometimes done with the manager's assessment, where the employee has a chance to read it before the meeting. Personally, I like the process of both assessments being done and exchanged ahead of time. That way the actual review meeting can often be more productive because there are - wait for it – no surprises."

"That sounds like a good process. Are there any downsides?"

"In my estimation, the only downsides are the extra time it might take to prepare and read the assessments prior to the meeting. Also, unfortunately I've seen situations in which the employee has done a self-assessment and the manager just 'lifts' input from the employee's comments without giving much thought to first doing a managerial assessment. I think that does a disservice to the potential dialogue."

"What if the employee and the manager are way off on their assessments?" Ariel asked.

"If they are, that could constitute a surprise. That would make me think they had not kept in communication about the what and how of the employee's performance throughout the year. One exception to that could be that the employee had worked with a different manager than the one doing the review, such as could happen with a transfer or change in personnel. That's why practices related to keeping open lines of communication and relevant documentation work best for everyone."

"I see. Isn't it possible that the employee and manager could agree on the what and the how, yet differ on the rating?"

What Does It Mean To Be A Manager?

"Yes. But now you've moved us to another aspect of the review process. For organizations that use a rating structure – and not all do – there are many different standards and purposes. Let's start with the purposes – First, there is the assumed desire that it's not enough to review performance. People expect a 'grade' to have a measure for what they've done. This can be useful to see one's own progress over time if the rating system is consistent over time and across the organization. A second factor - a rating can be useful in comparing one employee's performance to others – again assuming consistency – and therefore can help in making decisions about compensation and potential promotions. Here again, there are differences between organizations. Some connect the performance review and ratings more-or-less immediately to rewards; others offset the reviews from compensation by as much as 6 months."

"Why would they do that?" Ariel wanted to know. "Wouldn't the review be more powerful if the rewards were more immediate?"

"There are a variety of reasons. The consequences of both the review and any compensation adjustment or promotion can help drive positive performance. Some studies have shown that some employees perform better a month or two before the review or potential compensation adjustment.

EVALUATE

Perhaps they consciously or unconsciously believe the manager will be most influenced by recent behavior as opposed to the full review cycle. Those studies also show that, if rewarded appropriately, the employee will perform better for a month or two after the review or compensation adjustment. So at most, these studies suggest, a review or reward can drive stronger performance for two to four months. Therefore, if the organization separates the review from the rewards by about 3 months, higher performance can be driven more effectively throughout the year. Many organizations shy away from quarterly reviews and rewards because of the time it can take, so they conduct the process either every 6 months or annually. What do you think about this, Ariel?"

"If the employee and manager have more frequent communication, every time they talk can help drive performance. I consider the formal review and any rewards as periodic recaps – with no surprises. But, I guess, I also have to follow whatever policies and procedures we have in my organization."

"OK. Let's look at a couple other reasons why rewards may not happen at roughly the same time as reviews. Some organizations conduct reviews all at the same time and attach compensation considerations to the budget cycle.

What Does It Mean To Be A Manager?

That can be a big hit depending on the size of the organization. So some stagger the reviews and/or compensation adjustments to smooth out the impact. Further, some organizations conduct reviews on the anniversary of a person's employment or promotion. Again, that may not coincide with the budget cycles. Here's another possibility: if one of the rewards is in the form of a promotion, in addition to budget planning, the promotion may need to wait until a suitable position is open."

"I'm getting a sense that there may be a long list of reasons for when to conduct reviews," sighed Ariel.

"Uh huh. And in my experience, there is no *one* right way, and some organizations change things up every once in a while. As you said, you just have to follow whatever policies and procedures you have in your organization."

"Well, let's go back a bit. This last part was about the timing of reviews and how closely connected they are to whatever rewards. We both agree that those practices depend on the organization's policies and procedures. What about the rating scales? It seems that those also differ from time to time."

"Say more about that," I encouraged.

EVALUATE

"When I've talked with friends in other organizations, generally I've heard of ratings in three broad categories – meets requirements, exceeds requirements, or does not meet requirements. I've also heard of ratings on a four-, five-, and seven-point scale for each specific goal or as an overall rating. Most of us wonder about the difference between a '3' and a '4', or similar. It can be very confusing."

"The better organizations provide definitions of each rating – no matter what the label or number. As we talked about before, these ratings can be defined on what the employee achieved and/or how it was achieved. Again, I don't believe there is just *one* right way, but I do believe, whatever the ratings are intended to measure, should have been clarified at the front end and throughout the review period."

"So there are no surprises," declared Ariel.

"Yes, and more than that. Reviews and rewards help drive performance effort. Each of us wants to know what's being measured and how. And more than that, we need to feel that the measurement process is relevant to what we've been asked to do, that the measurements are a true reflection of our performance, that the assignment of a rating is fair, and that any rewards are appropriate with respect to what we think everyone else is receiving and the organization's budget priorities. If the employee feels any of these things are not handled appropriately, she may say 'why bother?' and performance can suffer."

"That's a lot to consider. No wonder this is a tough task for many managers."

"OK. That's been a lot on the administrative aspects of performance evaluation. Going back to our original list of possible topics, what do you want to talk about next?"

"I'd like to go back to preparation and talk through how to structure the review conversation."

"OK. What are some of your thoughts about how to do that?"

"I'm back to purpose, process, and payoff. I want to start the conversation being sure we're on the same page about why we're meeting. And, that would be to review the employee's performance – both what and how – for the entire review period. In my case, that will be a full year. And, part of the purpose is to continue to build on our relationship as well as agree on what went well, where there are opportunities for continued improvement, and, again in my case, to assign a rating that will be used by top management to determine compensation adjustments."

"Sounds good. And the process?"

"I want to help us both be calm and candid. I will acknowledge there should be no surprises. More specifically, since I did ask each employee to do a self assessment, I'd like to start by having her walk me through each of her goals and describe what she accomplished and how. I'll use my communication skills to actively listen without judgment and clarify and confirm my understanding of what she's said. I want her to feel like I really heard her entire story before I go into my perceptions. Is it OK to take notes during this?"

"I think so. It can convey that you're listening. It can also be distracting if she wonders what you are writing – and why only sometimes. I recommend suggesting you both take notes to help ensure you don't miss any important pieces you may want to discuss further."

"OK. Then, after she's walked me through her entire assessment, I'll walk her through mine. I think, wherever I agree with her, I'll state that I agree and perhaps add a specific example or two, especially as positive reinforcement. And on that point, anywhere we disagree shouldn't be a surprise. In fact, if we've done well throughout the year in our communication, there is less likelihood of disagreements at all."

"That would be ideal. Sometimes that will happen, and sometimes the employee or you may mis-remember or intentionally distort the history in order to justify a certain rating. Be careful with that on either side."

"Yes. The process has to feel honest and fair," Ariel stated. "You know, Dad, talking about it like this makes it feel kind of stilted. I want to create a free-flowing dialogue."

"How might you do that?"

"I think I'd prefer to go one goal at a time to hear her take on what and how she did, then share my feedback. We can have a freer give and take that way."

"Once again, there is not *one* right way. And, for whatever reason, you may want to do it differently with different employees. The point here is for you to have thought through how you intend to do it and communicate that with the employee at the beginning so there's less confusion about who's talking about what and when."

EVALUATE

"OK. Let me think – what else needs to be in this discussion?" Ariel thought aloud.

"Oh, a part of the process should include what the next steps will be. This probably differs from one organization to another, but here, I have to submit all my assessments and recommended ratings to upper management before I inform any employee of her rating. This way, management surveys all the input and recommendations across the organization to ensure some degree of consistency and determine potential merit increases and possible bonuses. It takes them about 2 weeks to go through everything and get back to me. After that, I'm able to 'negotiate' anything about the ratings or compensation adjustments before informing the employee of their final rating and compensation adjustment."

"It's good that you're clear on how things work in your organization. Be sure to clarify some of that with your employees so they have an understanding of what will happen and when."

"Of course. But even if I try to do that, a lot about how top management determines the compensation adjustments is just a mystery to me."

"It is to many of us – even top management in some cases.

What Does It Mean To Be A Manager?

Let me try to give you a few things that are typically factored into the decisions. One is how the overall organization performed financially, especially when compared to its budget forecasts. Usually, there must be a profit in order to afford to support pay increases, but not always. In some larger organizations, top management may also consider how well particular units performed and allocate more or less monies accordingly. Eventually it gets down to the individual contributor, and based on that person's performance – the what and how - a specific rating is determined and along with that a commensurate compensation adjustment. This is usually referred to as a 'merit increase' because the employee *earned* the results achieved."

"Oh yeah. I've also heard some organizations might give a 'cost of living increase'. That's generally a set percentage across the board no matter what a person's position or specific achievements. It just helps people keep up with inflation. Right?"

"Generally, but a lot more can go into that calculation. For example, many organizations have access to surveys that indicate ranges of pay for various kinds of positions in different industries and markets. Those surveys suggest a low, middle, and high range. Some organizations have a strategy around the talent levels of who they want to attract and retain and may intend to stay near, below, or above the middle of the ranges. The financial value of a job – separate from the person – may change over time, so you may hear of someone who's paid at the top of their range. In some cases, an organization may freeze' a person's pay raises until and if that individual is doing a role that justifies being in a higher range. They may still get whatever cost of living increase, but perhaps little or no merit increase."

"Somehow that doesn't sound fair," protested Ariel. "If the employee is doing the complete job and achieving the required results, shouldn't she be entitled to a merit increase?"

"Again, this will vary depending on the organization and its strategies. As harsh as this might sound, I believe every job – not the person – but every job has a limit on the value it adds to the organization, financially or otherwise. When the person reaches that top value of the job, she needs to grow beyond the position to provide more value or accept that she's likely not to get much in the way of merit increases."

"That still doesn't seem right!" Ariel protested again. "But I can see where even with my role, it's only so valuable *financially*. I want to do this role the very best I can, but I can see where some people might say it's not *financially* as valuable as the CEO's job. Did you hear my emphasis on *'financially'*?" she asked.

"Yes I did. And when it comes to compensation, much of the value of a person's job – again, not the person – is based on the perceived financial value. You and I both know there's much more to the value of a job than its financial contribution and that there is no upper limit to the potential additional value an individual can bring to the role. But, we're talking about compensation right now."

"OK, I'll back off a bit. What about bonuses? I know some people get a bonus in addition to or instead of a merit increase or cost of living increase."

"Another can of worms in some cases," I laughed. "Very generally, organizations that pay bonuses to a select group or to everyone usually base that on measurable outcomes that exceed the forecasted targets. If the organization does well in a given time period, they may chose to reward the over-and-above results across the organization, by specific units, or by individual achievements. In lean times, some organizations choose to give a bonus as a compensation adjustment rather than increasing the base salary. That way they can avoid getting 'locked in' and struggle to provide an increase the next round based on higher base salary levels.

EVALUATE

Many organizations are moving toward a kind of 'pay for performance' practice to more directly reward people for what they've actually achieved versus what a survey suggests should be the salary range. It's a hotly debated topic."

"Well, I could argue several points on that, too, I'm sure. But, thanks for clearing up some of the mystery. I'll try to leave that all in the proverbial 'black box' when I'm doing performance reviews."

"Sorry if I added complexity and confusion. What, if anything else, would you like to talk about with respect to the evaluate task of management?"

"Two more things, I think. One is about goal setting for the next review period. I think we've covered that a lot back in the formulate, articulate and initiate tasks. I just need to recycle through that process. The other is about what the employee should focus on learning and being able to do in the next review period. And, as I think about it, we discussed that earlier as well regarding the training phase and my task to educate. So I guess my question is whether these pieces should be a part of the review conversation."

"What is your experience or ideas about it?"

What Does It Mean To Be A Manager?

"Oh, when will I ever learn that I won't get a straight answer from you when I first ask something?" sighed Ariel with a lilt in her voice. "It depends! It's somewhat situational and somewhat determined by the practices of our organization. My preference would be that we have two separate conversations. One is looking backward to review what's been accomplished and learned. The other is looking forward at what's next to be done and what needs to be learned to do it. Sometimes, it's easier to just move from one conversation to the next due to time constraints. I'd prefer to do them with time in between so we can be really clear on the purpose of each conversation."

"I agree, if it's possible. Also, the review conversation isn't really over yet. From what you described in your organization, it may take a couple weeks of top management study before you can really complete the review conversation. On the other hand, it's important to get the next performance period clarified and moving forward. Just be clear about the purpose and process of whatever you're talking about so there will be ..."

"No surprises!" exclaimed Ariel. "I think you've made that point."

"OK. I know you have a number of these conversations

coming up over the next few weeks. Good luck. Let me know if you want to talk further during the process or to debrief afterwards. Love you."

"Thanks Dad. Love you, too."

Chapter 13: PARTICIPATE – Part 4

It was the middle of the afternoon about three weeks after Ariel and I had talked about the formal performance reviews she was about to conduct. I was working in my office putting the final touches on a proposal for an important client. The client needed the proposal by end-of-day so they could take it to the Board tomorrow for approval. We'd gone back and forth a few times and I knew I needed only about 20 minutes to complete it.

My phone rang – and I chose to let it ring. A quick glance showed that the call was from Ariel. I figured it could go to voicemail. If she had something more urgent, I knew she'd call back again very soon, and I could answer it then. I lightly chastised myself for even having the ringer on and not immediately directing calls to voicemail. Any distraction, no matter how fleeting, took my mind off the important task and deadline I was working on.

Shortly, the light blinked indicating she had left a voicemail. I heaved a mental sigh of relief that whatever she had was probably not as important or urgent as finishing the proposal. I would get back to her within half an hour.

After 15 minutes I finished my proposal revisions and sent them off to the client. I had to check a few emails and voicemails that had come, but nothing pressing. The one from Ariel: "Hi Dad. Nothing urgent. I just want to give you an update on the performance reviews and get your input on something that seemed to be a theme. Almost everyone – myself included – commented on how much we have to get done, how hard we're working, and the need for better time management. Call me when you get a chance. Ironically, I'll be in and out of numerous meetings over the next couple days so it may be hard to reach me."

I smiled to myself. Time management – the bane of so many of us – is rearing its ugly head and possibly distracting

What Does It Mean To Be A Manager?

her from the real issue – priority management. I was eager to see where our conversation might go. I sent her a text message with some available times so she could look at it when she was able and choose what might work. Another full day passed before we were able to connect with sufficient time to talk.

"Sorry it took a bit of time to connect'" she apologized. "I guess that probably indicates I have a time management challenge," she laughed, though I could hear the stress in her voice. "But before we get into that, let me just tell you that the performance review process went fairly smoothly and was actually easier than I thought regarding the actual conversations. The upper management review was not too painful and I probably was supported on about 95% of my recommendations for ratings. The compensation adjustments were in line with my expectations and my employees were generally pleased with their merit and cost of living increases. So, thanks again for your help on that stuff."

"You're welcome," I replied, recognizing that it was her hard work that produced the results. "In your voice mail and at the beginning of this call, you suggested that you and your employees are challenged with time management. Tell me more about that."

"OK. About the time we started the review conversations a few weeks ago, we also got the go ahead on some additional projects that will have a great, positive impact on our clients," she hesitated, "… if we do them well. We all seem to be really excited about the potential, but we have so much other work that is still on our plates. Everyone is feeling stressed with how much there is to do or that we don't have enough people to get all the work done at the quality level we desire. I've had several employees come see me to ask how it's possible to do everything we have to do."

"And your responses so far?" I asked.

"I've had several different ones depending on how overwhelmed I was feeling and who I was talking to. Generally, I've been saying things like 'it'll get better soon' or 'hang in there' or that really uncomfortable comment, 'I appreciate what you're doing. We'll just have to work harder'. It's really frustrating. Even with the time management tools for managing blocks of time on our calendars, being better organized, removing distractions from our lines of sight, more efficient meetings, and so on, it still seems impossible to get everything done." She sounded exasperated.

"Perhaps you're trying to solve the wrong problem," I calmly

What Does It Mean To Be A Manager?

suggested.

"What's that mean?!" she asked.

"Let me tell you a quick story. There once was a mighty group of soldiers on the field of battle slogging across a rain-soaked field. The commander ordered his troops to grab ladders and ascend a wall that was in front of them. Like good soldiers, they placed their ladders against the wall and put in their best efforts to climb to the top. Some of the rungs were missing. Some of the ladders were slippery and many kept falling back, even knocking into their comrades and many having to start over. They kept working as hard as they could until finally the commander himself made it to the top rung to peer over the wall so he could determine their next actions. What he saw was that the real battle was off in a different direction. The soldiers still scrambling below shouted up to the commander to get a status report – to hear how well all their hard work of slogging across the field and climbing the ladders had paid off. Finally the commander called out – 'Wrong wall!'"

"Ha!" responded Ariel. "I wonder if that's what we're doing – or if there are just too many walls to climb."

"A commander - let's say manager - must be careful of

what's called 'the activity trap'. It's important to work hard, but put the effort into the right things. You need to be sure you're working smarter, not harder. "

"That sounds like a good cliché, but how do I determine what the right things are, especially with so many to choose from?"

"Ariel, it may in fact be the case that you and your team need to practice some better time management. First, though, I think it would be helpful to figure out what are the different priorities regarding what needs to be done." I paused. "Do you have a list of all the various projects and tasks that need to get done?"

"Of course. You know me. I've got lists of lists."

"And how do you decide what to do first?"

"I look at the list every day – sometimes several times a day. But usually, first thing in the morning I'll update the lists to figure out how to spend my time – or direct others to spend their time. Sometimes, new things get added, especially from a client or a higher-level manager. In those cases, it's the squeaky wheel that gets the grease. Other times it's whatever came in first, especially if we've started on it. We

---

try to get that done because it's been sitting the longest. And, honestly, there are times we choose to work on something because it's just a little thing or perhaps fun, and we just want to get a sense of accomplishment. We always seem to be juggling too many balls."

"OK – let's talk through a way to possibly prioritize your list," I started.

"Oh – I also indicated 'high', 'medium' or 'low' every time I look at the lists. So I do consider priority to some extent."

"That's a beginning. How do you determine whether something is high, medium or low?"

"Well – you got me there. It's pretty much what I said a few moments ago about squeaky wheels, older projects waiting to get done, or quick, fun things. Not really a lot of thought."

"What you're describing is often the way people get things done. They make lists and indicate high, medium, and low. Sometimes it works fine. Other times, it might be helpful to dig a little deeper."

"I'm listening. Let's have it."

"So, let's start with a four-quadrant model."

"Of course," she snickered.

"Under the bottom horizontal line, write 'important'. Along the left side next to the vertical line, write 'urgent'. By the way, when I use the word 'urgent', I mean things that need a quick turnaround time, not necessarily that they are a crisis. Now indicate a scale on each axis from low to high. So, the upper right quadrant will be those things that are both important *and* urgent. Let's call that 'Priority 1'. The upper left quadrant will be things that are urgent, but not as important. These may be your squeaky wheels. Let's label those as 'Priority 2'. The lower right quadrant are things that are important, but not as urgent. Label those as 'Priority 3'. And finally, the lower left quadrant are things that are lower in importance and urgency, but you need to keep them on your radar."

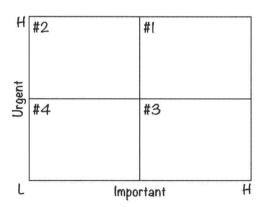

What Does It Mean To Be A Manager?

"I've seen a similar model in time management where whatever is in the lower left should just be taken off the list'" Ariel commented.

"For time management, I think that's appropriate. There are things that shouldn't even be listed. In this model, consider that whatever is in Priority 4 is important enough that at some point it will likely move into one of the other quadrants – and that can happen suddenly. For me, getting a new laptop was way down in Priority 4 – that is, until the day mine crashed! I'd been meaning to do some research – Priority 3 - for a someday purchase. The crash quickly jumped my computer need to Priority 1. "

"I get it. So I have the 4 quadrants. Now what?"

"You could simply take your To-Do List and spread all the items out across the four quadrants. And, if you're like many people I've worked with, your immediate thought might be most or all are Priority 1. So I impose an arbitrary rule. For whatever time frame you're considering – just what to do today, this week, this month, this quarter, or your life – you can never have more than 5 things in Priority 1! You can have fewer, but never more than 5. I call it the High 5. That means, you can't move something else in there until you either complete that item or intentionally swap it out for another item that is more important and more urgent. Sometimes that's where the squeaky wheel can move into Priority 1 and something else has to move out."

"That's harsh!" Ariel laughed. "But I can see how it might work. I *really* have to consider what 5 things are most important and urgent to work on."

"So here's a further tip to help you prioritize. For each task you consider putting into Priority 1, ask yourself, 'Who is this important to and why?' and 'When does that person *need* it – not just when do they *want* it, but *really* need it?"

"I can see where those two questions can certainly help determine which things have to be Priority 1. And I'm remembering our earlier discussion of the ABCs. I need to consider possible consequences if a particular item didn't make it to Priority 1 and get completed."

"Right. And the antecedents are important to everyone's success. Help the people who ask things of you to consider how and when they make their requests. Help them understand what else you have in Priority 1 and how that may impact when you can get to their request. As the saying goes, 'Their lack of planning shouldn't be a crisis for you'."

What Does It Mean To Be A Manager?

"I doubt I'd say that, but I get your point."

"OK. To go a bit further on that path, if you make a list of those 5 things that have to get done today, you don't leave until they are complete."

"Whoa! Now I'm into time management again! How can I get all 5 of my Priority 1 tasks done in a single day with everything else going on?"

"First general rule: break bigger tasks into smaller tasks. The entire project may be a Priority 1 over the next few weeks. What part of it will be Priority 1 today? What part tomorrow? And so on. Second general rule: estimate how much time each Priority 1 task will take and block that out on your calendar to be sure you have sufficient time to complete it."

"That's where the time management will come in. I have to block things out in 15 – 30 minute segments. That's about as long as I can go with a do-not-disturb sign on my door, email, or phone. "

'When you're clear on what Priority 1 task you're going to focus on without interruption, you'll be amazed how much you can get done of the right things. You'll be working smarter, not harder. You'll be much more able to accomplish your High 5 Priority 1 things each day."

"And, I suppose, with all this increased efficiency working on the right things – the most important and time-sensitive things – I might even check things off the list or move additional items into Priority 1 as time allows."

"As long as you don't go over 5 things at any one time."

"Now it's making sense. I have to try this out and then share what's working with the rest of the team. I think you're right. It's not so much about time management as it is priority management," Ariel said.

"One more question, Dad. What happens to all those things that don't seem to ever get to my Priority 1, but still need to get done?"

"Ah, that's where the management task of delegation might enter the picture."

"Well, hold off on that for now. Priority management is in my Priority 1 quadrant and I have some tasks to complete with that before I take on any more."

"You're absolutely right. Let me know how it goes and when you want to talk more."

"OK. Thanks, Dad. Bye for now."

DELEGATE

Chapter 14: DELEGATE

Over the next few weeks, Ariel and I talked about many things other than work, or just the quick update to report things were running fairly smoothly. Her no-longer-new employee, Sue, was through her training and was clearly in the sustaining phase of her employee cycle. Others were doing well also, having the normal ups and downs of performance. Ariel had been having regular one-to-ones with everyone and another quarterly team exercise where they completed some teamwork challenge exercises and had strong debriefs with immediate applicability to their on-the-job collaboration. Most were using their insights from the

What Does It Mean To Be A Manager?

personality styles work and Johari window along with basic communication skills and the ladder of inference to have focused problem-solving discussions, checking out assumptions as well as facts to be sure they were scaling the right walls.

Ariel was genuinely pleased with the team and each individual's performance. She was also pleased with her own learning and application of the various tasks of management we had discussed.

I was not surprised when on this call, after a general personal update and comments about how things were proceeding at work, she said, "Dad, last time when we had an in-depth conversation about management, we talked through the priority matrix. I had a lot of quadrant 1 work to do and to help my team members get clear on their priorities as well. We all seem to have a better handle on our work loads, yet I'm concerned that there are some things in my quadrants 2, 3 and 4 that haven't made it to my quadrant 1 and need some attention."

"That's pretty normal, Ariel. We all have to keep monitoring priorities and be sure to get the most important and urgent things done. Have you been able to get to some of the lower priority tasks at all?" I asked.

"Just a bit. And that's what I wanted to talk about. Last time you said that things that don't seem to ever get to my Priority 1, but still need to get done, is where the management task of delegation might enter the picture."

"Ariel, in my experience, doing a good job of delegation is one of the most challenging tasks of management. If done poorly, an employee may feel that she is being dumped on and become overwhelmed with what may seem like less-significant tasks. If done well, an employee will hopefully understand what the task is, why it's important, and why she was specifically chosen for the assignment. And, delegation done well can be extremely energizing by giving an employee more variety, challenge and responsibility."

"Sounds good to me," Ariel responded eagerly.

"OK. Let's start by going back to something you've said a few times. Generally your employees are doing well – that is, performing at or slightly above or slightly below their target performance level. Right?"

"That's right, even with the increasing expectations of working smarter and being able to produce greater results over time."

What Does It Mean To Be A Manager?

"So, let's focus on Sue again. Did you delegate tasks to her when she started working for you?"

"No – I just needed her to learn and do her job. While she was in her training phase, I just had her focus on the basics to get her job done."

"Hold that thought for a moment. How about over time, did you assign her new or additional work?"

"Of course. As she continued learning and getting the desired results, there was more work for her to do that was part of her job."

"How did she seem to take on the first and additional tasks as you assigned them to her?

"Willingly. She understood that the assignments were part of the process to help her get up to the target performance level and then sustain her performance over time with an ever-increasing skill set and higher expectations. She also understood how the work she was doing contributed to the organization's results."

"How is what you did to get her up to speed and performing at higher levels different from your idea of delegation?" I prodded.

"Oh," she said with a thoughtful pause. "Well, I guess in a way it was delegation. But I usually think of delegation as assignments that are above and beyond the normal responsibilities of the specific job."

"Most people do. However, I want you to hear yourself as you described some aspects of what you've been doing all along with Sue. Some of the tasks you assigned to her were specific to helping her learn her job or to increase her skills and knowledge. Some tasks were assigned as you saw she was able to meet ever-higher expectations. It sounds like you also helped her understand that the assignments weren't just 'make work' – or perhaps just taking things off your plate to put on hers – but were genuinely important contributions to organization results."

"Yep – I did all that", Ariel agreed proudly. "I get it that I've been delegating all along things that are part of Sue's job."

"I consider the type of delegation you've been doing is a normal part of participating with an employee in the sustaining phase of their performance. It's important to note that employees remain in the sustaining phase for various amounts of time, some for their entire career with an organization. They consistently do their job at or near the ever-increasing target performance level, have various assignments delegated to them that are closely related to their job responsibilities, and get feedback, recognition and rewards commensurate with their contribution to organization results. This is traditionally true of the majority of employees and is extremely valuable to the organization and it's clients. And further, this consistent sustaining of performance seems in alignment with what the employee wants or needs to be fully integrated and motivated in both work and her life."

"I agree," said Ariel. "And, I know there are many – myself included – who are hungry for more. I want to keep learning and growing, take on more challenges and responsibilities, and have more opportunities to make a greater impact within and beyond my organization. I think that's true of most - but not all of my employees - and Sue is clearly there. She's been asking what else she can do."

"Terrific! When an employee has been in their sustaining phase for awhile – again the time may vary – and she is performing consistently above the target performance level of her job, she is moving into what I call the Gaining phase. In this phase, the delegate task of management expands from what you've been doing all along."

"OK. That's the kind of delegation I want to learn more about. I've got stuff that needs to get done and Sue and others certainly seem ready to step up."

"Ariel, I hear you are eager to delegate – at least some things to some people. Before we go there, I'm wondering if you've ever experienced hesitancy on the part of a manager to delegate, even if they seem to be aware of the need?"

"I sure have. In a previous job, I felt I was ready and able to take on more and said so to my manager. He seemed to be very reluctant to give up much beyond mundane tasks. It's part of the reason I eventually left. And I have friends who have expressed similar frustrations."

"What might be some reasons some managers may be hesitant to delegate?"

"Interesting question. Let's see. As we've done in our conversations before, I'll use the male pronoun to refer to a manager, although we both know that these things are not gender specific. So, *he* may be hesitant to delegate because he doesn't believe someone else can do the task at all, or at least as well as he can. He doesn't want to give up control. Even if he thinks someone else can do the task, he may be uncomfortable that it may feel like dumping extra work on someone whose plate is already full. Those kinds of things."

"Great. And what else?"

"He may just really enjoy a particular task and not want to give it up. Or he may like being seen as the hero and not want to share the limelight. Or, and I've heard this one before, he may hesitate to delegate because the employee would expect an increase in pay for doing extra work."

"That comment deserves more exploration, but we'll hold it for now. Anything else?"

"He may be concerned that he'll still have to be closely involved – or even take over the task again. He might feel it could take more time and effort to delegate a task than to just do it himself, especially if it's a one-time thing."

"And …?"

"He may be concerned if someone else can do the task, that means he is less important. He may see not delegating as job security. I certainly had that experience," Ariel sighed.

"I'd be really concerned with that belief, because it means he can't move on to other things. He may be thinking about job security as keeping others out, but it may serve to lock him in."

"That's certainly not my problem. I have so many other things I want and need to do, I'm eager to delegate to have time to put in on other important things."

"OK, let's use that as a segue. In addition to having time to do other important things, why else might a manager *want* to delegate?"

"Well, time is the biggest thing for me! I've been putting in longer hours and taking more work home. So that's enough right there for me to want to delegate," Ariel stated emphatically. "I think some other reasons to delegate might be to provide further training and development for an employee - to build the overall capacity of the team. It could even be an opportunity for an employee to demonstrate that they are ready for more variety, challenge and responsibility in preparation for a possible promotion."

"Right. What might be some other reasons to delegate?"

"Some employee may already have experience handling that kind of task so, especially if it's an urgent task, she could perhaps get it done faster or better than the manager. And again, from my own experience, I was the one familiar with a particular case and the various people involved, so it would have made more sense for me to go further than for my manager to step in and take over."

"So, a manager may want to delegate to gain more time, to provide for continued professional development, to increase team capacity, and because someone might already have applicable experience or be closer to the task. That's a good list of reasons to start with," I summarized.

"Oh – and here's probably a poor reason, but I've experienced this one, too. The manager may feel he's just got to get the task off his plate and grabs a warm body to give it to. When that happened to me a few times, I felt the message was that what I was already working on wasn't very important or that my manager didn't care about how much time I had to put in with the extra workload."

I could tell Ariel was reliving some difficult memories of poor management. "You're absolutely right. That's when it feels like dumping. However, there may be times that a manager has good reasons for delegating such tasks – like the need for more time. So we'll revisit that when we talk further about what to delegate to whom and how. Are you OK to move on?" I asked gently.

"Yeah. That felt good to say those things so I can be more aware of the good reasons for delegating and beware of how it may come across to my employees if I'm not careful."

"Good. So let's switch to considering what tasks could be delegated. Let's start with a somewhat generic list. Later, you could go through the tasks you have in priority quadrants 2, 3, and 4 to make a more-specific list of possibilities. So, what are some general tasks that you typically do? On what do you spend your time?"

"Just off the top of my head – report writing, reviewing documents, attending meetings, writing proposals, talking to clients, working with other management people, funders, vendors, assigning work, reviewing work, coaching, general supervising, creating and overseeing the budget, performance reviews. It feels like an endless list."

"And just to add to the list – what else could or should you be doing that you haven't felt able to get to?"

"Gee Dad. Thanks for reminding me!" Ariel laughed. "Well there's strategic and long-term planning, further coordination with other organizations serving our clients, looking at the

What Does It Mean To Be A Manager?

systemic causes of the problems we try to solve so we can partner to find ways to prevent the root causes, paying more attention to my own professional growth. Little stuff like that!"

"OK. I might ask you, 'Of all those things, what could you delegate to someone else, assuming the right person can be identified and has time?' However, let me ask a different question. Of all those things, what could you NOT delegate to someone else?"

"I like the first question better. It seems like it would be easier to figure that out. But ... what couldn't I delegate? I think as I get into more supervisory and managerial tasks, I would have to do those myself. I couldn't have anyone else do performance coaching, assign work, review work, do budgets, and especially not conduct performance reviews."

"OK. I agree with you that many of the general tasks you listed can be more easily delegated. You can pass on some responsibility and authority for doing them, and still retain ultimate accountability. So let's take a look at each of the others you listed as needing to be done by you. Let's start with performance coaching. Is it possible a more experienced employee could provide some coaching to a less experienced one?"

"Of course! Before I became a manager, I did a lot of that. And here I had some other employees work with Sue as she was in her training phase." Ariel paused. "OK – at least some performance coaching can be delegated. I just have to be sure I'm making the right matches for the right reasons."

"OK – and assigning and reviewing work?"

"As long as we all know the big picture and end results, there are times I have asked some employees – and even other managers - to review work and recommend further assignments. I could probably do more of that – again with the right matches – and still keep tabs on what's going on."

"Budgets?" I asked.

"I can get input on parts of it, but the organization doesn't want to share all the numbers, even with me. And it's my neck on the line if we mismanage, especially with how tight things are."

"Other than organization policy and norms, is budget management a skill someone could learn and do well over time?"

What Does It Mean To Be A Manager?

"Sure – that's part of how I got the job I have. Someone else *could* do it, but I don't believe it would be allowed."

"OK – and performance reviews?"

"Probably the same as budgets. Someone else could do them; but I don't believe it would be allowed in the organization. Besides, on-going coaching and performance reviews are a great way to stay connected to what and how everyone is doing. That's a big part of my job and I really enjoy it."

"Another quick story. Back in the 90's – that's the *1990s!* – I was a manager in a department of 120 employees. We organized in self-directed work teams and by projects. Each team was responsible for interviewing and selecting people to be on their team, for assigning and reviewing work, for managing their budgets, and for conducting performance reviews including rarely-overturned recommendations for ratings and compensation adjustments. I oversaw everything and was held accountable by top management, but the supervisory and management tasks were done in the teams. There were designated lead people by project, but no one else who was consistently and only in a management role. What I learned – and want you to consider – is that there is virtually *nothing* that I could not delegate." I paused.

DELEGATE

"So, given that, it may come back to organization policy and procedures about what you should *not* delegate, but everything else is possible."

"Oh my! That can really open up some possibilities – and a can of worms. I'll have to think about all that."

"Then, this is probably a good time to take a break. I'd like to suggest a homework assignment. Go through your general list of tasks that could be delegated along with specific tasks you have in quadrants 2, 3 and 4, and make a more-specific list of tasks for possible delegation. In preparation for our further work on this, I suggest you create a spreadsheet labeled 'Delegation Possibilities' with these tasks listed in the first column. Are you willing to do that?"

Delgation Possibilities	
Possible Tasks	

"Absolutely. And I'll have it done by the end of this week so we can talk about it over the weekend – say Sunday afternoon about 4?"

"Great. I look forward to it. Take care. Love you."

"Love you too, Dad. And thanks."

DELEGATE - Part 2

Chapter 15: DELEGATE – Part 2

It was mid-afternoon Sunday and I was anxiously awaiting
Ariel's call. I knew that she had really got it with respect to
reasons to delegate and would have a long list of
possibilities. There would be three more probable
discussions to help her work her way through to continuous
good delegation practices, and I knew that most managers
didn't like the detail and analytical work I was planning to
share with her, preferring to give cursory consideration and
then go with their gut – or do nothing. I was hopeful that Ariel
would put in the effort. Since she was very little, she had put
in a lot of effort when sorting and re-sorting everything from

What Does It Mean To Be A Manager?

crayons to Barbie dolls.

Right on schedule the call came at 4 pm. We caught up on a few personal things – Mom's work and community volunteer efforts with the housing board, my upcoming guitar concert, her sister's party, her brother's new job. She shared about her quilting activities and youth work at church. After a while, others left the call and Ariel said, "That was a lot of work just making a list of tasks to possibly delegate. Just doing that was both overwhelming and liberating!"

"How so?" I asked.

"It's amazing how much there is to do – and, the possibility of getting more of it done through delegation rather than on my own really got me thinking. Every time I caught myself saying, 'I can't delegate that' I kept asking, 'Why not?' I don't expect to delegate everything, but at least it's on my list for consideration."

"Good job, Ariel! Ready for the next step?"

"Let's do it!" she exclaimed. "I've got my 'Delegation Possibilities' spreadsheet right here."

"OK. Again, with what sounds like a long list, I'll just help you think through a few considerations. It will be up to you how much you do with the entire list, but at least you'll have some tools. So, first question about your list – did you think about or identify how important or urgent each task is?"

"Yep – I did some of that. especially as I transferred some tasks from my own priority matrix. One thing I was thinking about though, is that the importance or urgency was based on my priorities. If I were to delegate the task, it might be in a different quadrant for the person I delegate it to."

"Great insight, Ariel. When we come back to it, that consideration will help you determine who to delegate a task to and how. For now, I recommend you use the second column next to each task to indicate the relative organization priority. In other words, which quadrant of the matrix would the task be in relative to the goals of the organization?"

Delegation Possibilities	
Possible Tasks	Organizational Priority

What Does It Mean To Be A Manager?

"A quick look suggests that most of them line up with my own priorities. That may be true, but I'll have to go over them all to be sure I'm not just biased."

"Good. So now that you have a list of tasks and their organizational priority, the next thing you might want to indicate is what special skills or knowledge may be needed to successfully complete the task. For some, you may think there's nothing special – that almost anyone could do the task; and for others, that there are a number of specific skills and knowledge that only a few people currently have."

"Oh. That will take some time. If it's my task, I usually already have the skills and knowledge or know what I need to do to get up to speed. But, if I take a little time, I can easily highlight the most critical aspects of what a task will take. And, since most of the skills and knowledge will be applicable for many tasks, I think I'll create a coded index so I can plug those codes into column 3," suggested Ariel.

"I like the way you think! That coding will come in handy in many ways very shortly and over time."

"Well, you know how I've always liked to sort things and create easy memory tools."

"I sure do," I affirmed as I smiled to myself.

Delegation Possibilities		
Possible Tasks	Organizational Priority	Special Skills and Knowledge (I)
...		
(I) See codes for special skills and knowledge		

"OK. Got it. Task. Organizational priority. Codes of skills and knowledge needed. What's next?"

"Terrific. Here comes the fun part. The who. Let's start with a general brainstorm again. What are some categories of people to whom you could possibly delegate a task?"

"That's obvious. My employees!"

"Yes, and who else?"

"Who else? No one else reports to me. There is no 'who else'!"

What Does It Mean To Be A Manager?

"Can you only delegate to people who report to you?" I prodded. Then, "Earlier you mentioned that you got some help from others regarding Sue's training."

"Well, I didn't delegate to them. I just asked for their help."

"OK. Call it what you will. But with that request for help in mind, what are some other possible categories of people to consider?"

"Well, now that we put it that way, I could ask for help from – or delegate to – employees in other departments. Perhaps my peers. Maybe even my boss."

"And who else?"

"Well, that's all the people inside the organization," she replied sounding a little exasperated again.

"If you thought 'outside the organization' – who else comes to mind?"

"OK – for some tasks, it's really the responsibility of the client to do some things for themselves. So I could 'delegate' to clients." She paused. "And, we have suppliers – vendors and consultants. Perhaps there are some things that could be delegated to them. And our other organizational partners – there are people in those organizations I could ask for help. I guess as I think about it, there is a pretty long list of people. I just have to be real careful who I ask to do what."

"Great. This exercise is to help you broaden your thinking. Other categories or specific people will probably come to mind as you go through your task list. You may not choose to delegate much beyond your immediate employees, but having thought it through, you may find greater opportunity and flexibility than you'd originally been thinking."

Delegation Possibilities			
Possible Tasks	Organizational Priority	Special Skills and Knowledge (1)	Who could do this? (2)
...			
(1) See codes for special skills and knowledge (2) Names of my employees, other employees, peers, boss, clients, suppliers, consultants			

What Does It Mean To Be A Manager?

"This helps. What's next?" Her enthusiasm was returning.

"I think it might be helpful to let this spreadsheet rest a few moments, and create another one. I call this one a 'capacity matrix'."

"Dad, you've got a tool and a name for everything!" she teased.

"It can seem that way," I laughed. "One responsibility of a manager is to ensure there is sufficient capacity in the employees – or others to whom they might delegate – to get all the important work done today and in the future. So this matrix will help you determine what your capacity is and how you might plan to develop it further."

"Sounds good."

"So, using a spreadsheet format again, let's go back to that compilation of skills and knowledge you were starting to create. Column 1 will be a complete list with space to add more of what it takes for any and all work done in your department. Don't try and complete it right now, but get a few down so you can remember this for later."

"OK. I listed six things right away. What's next?"

DELEGATE - Part 2

"Across the top, create a row for the name of each employee or other potential delegatee. For now, it might be easiest to stick with your employees. And, while you're at it, provide 2 columns below each name. The first of those columns will be that employee's current level of expertise – high, medium or low – for each skill. Label that column 'Now'. The second column is to indicate a future level of expertise you will need from that employee, perhaps in 6 months or a year. For our purposes at the moment, let's think in terms of 6 months. So label that column '6 months'.

I waited as she filled in some names and headings. Then, "Let's work through a couple examples. What's one of the skills or knowledge categories you listed?"

"Use our Excel template to track client meetings. Almost everyone has to do that."

"OK. Let's consider Sue as an example. Given that skill, how well does Sue do it now – high, medium or low?"

"Well, she's still new on this but seems to be getting the hang of it. I'll give her a 'medium'. I put an 'M' in the first column under her name next to that skill."

"And where do you need her to be in 6 months?"

What Does It Mean To Be A Manager?

"By then she needs to be at a 'High' level – 'H'," announced Ariel. "And, that was just *using* the template. The next skill is to *create* Excel spreadsheets. She's a 'low' now and I just want to get her up to 'medium'. That won't be a critical part of her job." She was now on a roll. "And as I think of it, another skill will be creating the actual templates for others to use. That's not planned to be something she will do in her current job. She's 'low' now, and can stay 'low' in the future."

"Sounds like you got the hang of it. Just start to fill in one more to be sure. Use the same three skills in relation to another employee."

"OK. Mary. On using the templates, she's 'high' and 'high'. On creating spreadsheets she's 'high' and 'high'. On creating templates, she's 'high' and 'high', but it's no longer a part of her job. Should I mark that last one down to 'low' or medium' because it's no longer a skill she needs to use in her work?"

"Great question. What are your thoughts?"

"Well, for Sue, I can clearly see opportunities for further development and relatively how critical each skill is. For Mary, I think it's helpful to see that she has the high level of skill even if it's not part of her job, because if I ever have to have someone create a template quickly, I could possibly delegate it to her."

Capacity Matrix		Sue		Mary		Ellen		Pamela		Dan	
Skills and Knowledge	Code	Now	6 mo	Now	6 mo	Now	6 mo	Now	6 mo	Now	6 mo
Use Excel template to track client meetings	E-TC	M	H	H	H						
Create Excel spreadsheets	E-CS	L	M	H	H						
Create Excel Templates	E-CT	L	L	H	H						
...											

"And, as you fill in the rest of the capacity matrix...?" I asked.

"I'll have the beginnings of a development plan for each individual and a quick resource of who I can turn to if I need the expertise immediately. This is another good one, Dad. Thanks."

"It has great potential and you'll need to keep it up to date as you add new skills and knowledge to the list and as people develop over time."

"I think that will be worth it. I might even delegate that task to someone else once I get it set up."

"OK. Now let's go back to the previous spreadsheet – 'Delegation Possibilities'. You've already created column 4 labeled 'Who could do this?' As you go through this, you may want to insert separate rows for each possible person. I'll leave that decision to you. So, pick a task off your list that you want to practice with."

"Ironically, one of those is to create an Excel spreadsheet for tracking expenses by client."

"Good. That should help us get the practice quickly. Given what we've already talked about, next to that task you would have indicated the relative organizational priority and the codes of the skills and knowledge needed to complete the task."

"All there. Now I'm listing possible people to whom I could delegate this task. For our purposes, let's just talk about Sue and Mary. Sue is low on the skills to do it but needs to learn how in the next 6 months. This could be a possible assignment for her. If I needed it quickly, I could delegate it to Mary who could knock it out right away."

DELEGATE - Part 2

"You're moving faster than I was, Ariel. So a suggestion might be, create a column 5 labeled 'Readiness', and next to each person's name use a 'T' to indicate someone would need training to do the task and an 'N' meaning the person can do it now."

"So Sue's a 'T' and Mary's an 'N'. I can see where this is going. By listing names of potential people to assign a given task along with their readiness to do it, I can get a good sense of who to possibly assign it to depending on urgency."

"Exactly – up to a point. Let's add one more column for your analysis. Column 6 labeled 'Why?' Remember when you were brainstorming possible reasons to delegate a task to someone?"

"Sure – to develop that person, to build team capacity, because that employee is closer to the situation, because the person has the skills and experience, and because I need time to work on other tasks. I'll add another – potential partnership. That's where it might make sense to leverage relationships beyond my direct reports. Oh, and we dismissed the reason to delegate just because the person is a warm body and happens to be available."

"Good memory! So all those – including warm body – are

possible reasons why you might select someone to do the task. Identifying those reasons on this spreadsheet will help you make the selection *and* help you when it's time to do the actual delegation."

"I may be jumping ahead again, but I think I'll use the following codes. 'D' for development; 'T' for team capacity; 'C' for close to the situation; 'E' for experienced with the kind of task, 'P' for partnership, and 'A' for availability. I'm not including a code for gaining more time for me, because that will probably be true of just about anything and wouldn't be enough of a reason by itself. What do you think?"

	Delegation Possibilities				
Possible Tasks	Organizational Priority	Special Skills and Knowledge (1)	Who could do this? (2)	Readiness (3)	Why (4)
...					

(1) See codes for special skills and knowledge
(2) Names of my employees, other employees, peers, boss, clients, suppliers, consultants
(3) Readiness: Now = N, With training = T
(4) Why: Development = D, Team Capacity = T, Close to Situation = C, Experienced with kind of task = E, Potential Partnership = P, Available = A

"Sounds like a great beginning. Of course, you own all this so you can adjust it anyway you think will serve you better over time."

"I would do that anyway, but thanks for the permission." I could hear her smiling again.

"OK. Please run me through it all again and how you might use it."

"Sure. I have a 'Delegation Possibilities' spreadsheet listing tasks that need to get done along with an indication of the relative organizational priority of each task. Further, I know what special skills and knowledge will be needed to complete each task and along with my 'Capacity Matrix' spreadsheet, I can easily see who has the current ability to do the task or could do it with some training. I have a list of possible people to whom I could delegate the task – including people who don't report to me – and an indication of possible reasons to delegate to any given person, including their availability. My next steps are to complete the spreadsheets and do some further analysis so I can start to delegate higher priority tasks to the right people for the right reasons."

"You've nailed it. I have one further consideration based on what we've discussed. I'm remembering the task of creating a spreadsheet for tracking expenses by clients. You said Sue needs to learn it and Mary could get it done quickly."

Ariel jumped in. "I can see where you're going with that. If the timing works, I could have Mary train Sue and kill two birds with one stone." She paused – "Although I don't like the idea of killing birds."

"You're appropriately leveraging your resources to build team capacity. Way to go!"

"Now I just have to make the choices and hand out the tasks. Piece of cake!"

"Not quite so fast. How you hand out the tasks is really critical. If you want, we can talk through some ideas on that in the next few days."

"Good idea. Let me flesh out these spreadsheets first, and I'll get back to you Wednesday evening," she suggested.

"I'm looking forward to it. Good luck."

"Thanks Dad."

Chapter 16: DELEGATE - Part 3

"Dad," she started, after we quickly went over personal updates, "this was a lot more time consuming *and* insightful than I had imagined. As I built out the capacity matrix, I had so many different kinds of skills and knowledge that we as a team need to utilize. It ranged from comparatively simple things like generating reports to more complex budget management to really complex things like communicating with clients who have really messy situations. I got a sense of how the more complex stuff is built upon the less complex so I can see pathways to development."

What Does It Mean To Be A Manager?

So," I responded, "it sounds like in addition to being able to select someone to do a task, you have a better idea of how to delegate strategically to continually increase the capabilities of your team."

"Absolutely! I also have a better understanding of why it's important not only who I select for a given task and why, but also how I have the actual delegation conversation. This piece is critical to the strategic aspects well beyond just getting a task done."

"Sounds great. Now, before we go further with how to have the conversation for strategic delegation, let's back up just a bit. Think about tasks you've assigned to Sue as she was in her training phase or early sustaining phase. Would you change any of the tasks or the ways you assigned them to her?"

"Interesting question. As I think about it, I already was thinking strategically when I formulated the position description and specific objectives and process of her on-boarding and initial training. We did actually discuss the what, how and why of that process with the overall intent to help her get up to the target performance level. Each task was clearly aimed at helping her learn her job and to achieve desired results. In hindsight, I was delegating strategically.

We just didn't discuss it that much."

"And the early part of sustaining – anything different?"

"Once Sue was up to speed, I backed off from specific training to more participating. Helping her think through how to achieve results and what information and resources she would need to accomplish her tasks. She knew I was always available to her and we did regular check-ins, but she was given more rope as she demonstrated competence and confidence."

"And how did the conversations change during assigning tasks and monitoring performance? I'm specifically wondering about the proportion of you making statements – such as directing her what to do – compared to questions – such as asking for her ideas for how to do things, or how to handle situations as they came up."

"Partly thanks to my conversations with you, over time I was more conscious about asking more questions rather than making statements. It was hard sometimes, because I knew the answers and wanted to jump in to speed the process along. But I knew that if I did that, she wouldn't learn how to think things through for herself, and that would mean I'd always have to be engaged at a micro level. My over-involvement could have prevented her growth and possibly have undermined her desire to do the work. Or, it might have 'trained' her that she could still have a job but didn't have to work hard because I would make all the decisions. I could have created a sense of entitlement and lower achievement. Thank goodness, I didn't create a monster!"

"You're right, the early ways a manager interacts with an employee in whatever position or task, sets a level of expectation for all future performance and levels of engagement."

"Sure – the ABCs again. My early involvement with Sue – first more training and then gradually asking more questions to help her 'own' her work, were antecedents to the positive behaviors and results she's now showing. Good job, Ariel!" she said congratulating herself.

"So, back to my earlier question - Would you change any of the tasks or the ways you assigned them to her?"

"Given where she was in her abilities and desires to get the job done, I think what and how I delegated was just fine. Am I missing something?"

"I don't think so. I just wanted to help you consider the

question. Now as she moves forward and continues sustaining her performance at the target performance level, you have more tasks to assign her that are still very focused on her normal role – nothing particularly extraordinary. Do you think you should continue to delegate and monitor as you have been doing, or if and when would something change?"

"At this time, I think mostly more of the same will be sufficient. And I can see this changing over time to some of our delegation conversations and monitoring being more strategic."

"What will be indications to you that it's time for a different kind of delegation conversation with her?"

"When she demonstrates that her performance is consistently above the target performance level. Or, when she says she wants more challenge and variety. Or, when I need her to step up and take on more because of the work we have to do, or from a strategic capacity point of view."

"So – to put it simply, when she moves into the gaining phase of performance – at least in some aspects – and there is an organizational need for her to take on more, then you'll be ready to delegate differently."

What Does It Mean To Be A Manager?

"Yes. And, I think we're there now. At least I have a particular assignment in mind that I believe would be good to give her. As I made up the list of possible tasks to delegate, I identified one that's been in my quadrant 3 for a while and needs to get done. As I used my delegation planning spreadsheet, Sue showed up as one of three people who made sense. This is a bit of a stretch for her so she'll get both variety and challenge. It will build her skill set in alignment with my capacity matrix. And, having just completed another task, she has the time to take this on now."

"Sounds like you've got all the makings of a good strategic delegation. So let's work through how to plan the conversation. Do you have sufficient clarity on what the task is and the outcomes needed by when?"

"Yes. And also why this task is important and who will be impacted by the results."

"Great. There is a much greater likelihood of success – getting what you need – when you can be clear about what, why, when, how and who. Next, it sounds like you are clear on why you are selecting her – more variety, challenge, specific skill development, and availability. So you'll want to include some or all of that in your conversation. You might also want to acknowledge what she already knows how to do that will help her with the assignment. That would be a good positive reinforcement."

"I'm comfortable with all that."

"Next, you might want to discuss what kind of support she may need from you or others to get the task done. This usually includes kinds of resources and what will be your level of engagement. What are some categories of resources that someone might need to complete any task?"

"Obviously that would vary depending on the task. But, generally, I think people need time, money, information, equipment, or other people. And, before you ask, by time I mean availability of sufficient time to get the work done by the due date, which may mean taking other things off their plate in the meantime. Putting other things in a different priority quadrant."

"Money?" I prompted her to continue on her list.

"Sometimes we will have already budgeted for a task or project. Other times we may have to reallocate or ask for more. For most of the tasks I identified, funds are already available – or it will stay as my task to get what's needed. I don't expect Sue to be able to get the funds – at least not yet or not for this task. That's still going to be my job." She paused. "I'm thinking I have to be careful with what and when I delegate a task if it's going to require more funds. I have to get those ducks in order before I give the task to someone."

"Most of the time, that's true. Sometimes there is preliminary work to do to demonstrate value, after which funding may be forthcoming. You mentioned 'information'. What's that mean?"

"Again, depending on the task, there could be some background information we have in house or some information that has to be collected from outside resources. I may have some information in my head that's not documented anywhere. So, we have to talk through what's available and how to get it so she isn't working in the dark or re-inventing the wheel."

"Right, unless gathering information is a part of the skill you need her to learn or improve. Then, you have to decide how much to provide or how much direction to give her." I was thinking about how important it is to be clear on what you want or need someone to learn and to balance that with getting the task done in the most expedient way. "Then you mentioned 'equipment'. What do you mean by that?"

"For most of what we have to get done, that is access to computers, printers, copiers, etc. I guess I'd throw in access to the internet for information gathering. Also access to our internal data bases and files of past reports and other documents. And," she laughed, "a workspace with a door for privacy when talking to clients face-to-face or over the phone."

I laughed, too, remembering when Ariel had a job involving a lot of confidential conversations. The office she had came without a door and there were many humorous attempts to find one that fit the oversized opening.

"Again, you could have all that planned out before you have the delegation conversation, or allow Sue to suggest what equipment and space she thinks she'll need. Part of your consideration again will be her learning versus expediency. Thinking through what's needed to get a task done is an important skill."

"And," said Ariel, "sometimes there is a need to have input or other interactions with other people. This task for Sue will only involve getting others' input. Some other tasks on my list will involve actually pulling together a work group and facilitating a collaborative effort to get the results. Lots of different skills will be needed there, especially when it involves people from other parts of the organization or outside."

"You might also consider if there is any need for clerical or administrative support. Would Sue be entering her own data and writing and editing her own reports? Will she need someone to run copies of anything? There are probably other people in the organization that already do those kinds of things. If and when should she ask them for assistance?"

"There will be lots of that kind of support needed. But, as I think of it, I've been the one to request that assistance, and because I'm a manager, things generally get done without question and in a timely manner. They may not do that for Sue."

"So ---?"

"So, I will have to talk to those people – or their boss – to be sure they understand that Sue is making requests on this task and to support her in the same efficient manner they've supported me. And, I guess that goes for anyone else she may be asking for input or other interaction. She'll be acting on my behalf."

"So you have to do some of what I call 'path clearing'. Some of that may be done prior to doing the delegation, part will be identified as you talk about the task, and some path clearing may be called for while the assignment is underway."

"Yep. So what else might I need to consider before I meet with Sue?"

"We've already talked a bit about Blanchard's model of Situational Leadership – matching your management style and activities to the level of readiness of the employee in terms of their ability and desire to do a task. We've also talked about some factors that may suggest you step up or hold back your involvement."

"I remember," Ariel said. "There could be factors such as visibility and political implications, financial considerations, urgency, complexity, and so on. Also, that it makes a difference how this delegation is balanced between a training goal and producing specific results."

"Exactly. So the question becomes one of the level of authority given to the employee to take action balanced with your desire and need to be involved."

What Does It Mean To Be A Manager?

"I'm sure you have a model for that, Dad," Ariel laughed.

"As a matter of fact - for this consideration, I really like a model I learned from my colleague Susan Scott in her book *Fierce Conversations*. She called it the Decision Tree. Imagine your organization as a tree. Decisions and actions that are crucial to the overall survival and growth of the tree are at the root level. As you move up the tree – trunk, branch, leaf - the decisions and actions are less critical, at least in the short term."

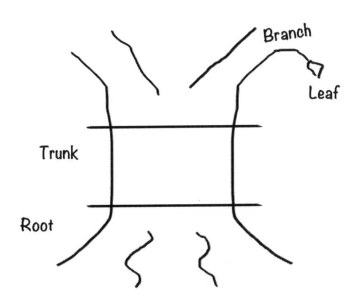

"OK. I'm following you."

"Now, when you delegate a task, you and the employee need to be clear on where it fits on the tree and how to handle decisions. Here is a way I like to say it. 'Sue, this portion of the task is at a *root* level. That means, if you come upon something that requires a decision, I want you to consider possible actions then come to me with your assessment and recommendations. Because it is a root-level consideration, I will make the decision on what happens next.'" I paused. "Or – 'Sue, this portion of the task is at the *trunk* level. That means, if you come upon something that requires a decision, I want you to consider possible actions then come to me with your assessment and recommendations. Because it is a trunk-level consideration' – and here's the critical part, Ariel – '*unless I disagree* because there are things you don't know, Sue, I will give you approval to move ahead with your recommendations'."

"Oh – so the difference between root and trunk is essentially, at the trunk, we'll move ahead with Sue's recommendations unless there was something missing. Right?"

"To be a bit more specific – trunk decisions are very important, but if a mistake is made, the organization can recover. There is a bit more space for taking a risk. You

What Does It Mean To Be A Manager?

may not fully agree with Sue's recommendations, but that doesn't mean they are wrong or won't work. Certainly you need to be clear on expectations, coach her around antecedents, draw out possible consequences, and so on. But in the end, unless you are sure what she's suggesting won't work or will be harmful to the organization, you would support her in taking the action she's suggested. This is what empowerment is all about. And for many managers, the hardest part of empowerment is letting go, even if you're not sure things will work out smoothly."

"OK – So, if things are at the trunk level, I want to coach Sue to think things through well, but also give her the authority to make the decision and take action after she's got my input. What's at the branch level?"

"Here's how it may sound – 'Sue, this portion of the task is at the *branch* level. That means, if you come upon something that requires a decision, I want you to consider possible actions then do whatever you think is best. After that, please close the loop with me to tell me about the situation and how you handled it.' And to continue - 'Sue, this portion of the task is at the *leaf* level. That means, if you come upon something that requires a decision, I want you to consider possible actions then do whatever you think is best. I don't need to hear about it, unless you want to bring it to my attention'."

"That seems clear. As I delegate an assignment, Sue and I need to agree on where the decisions fit on the tree and the commensurate levels of authority and my involvement. I like this model."

"Great. One further point – more as an obvious reminder. In addition to the clarity for delegation, the Decision Tree also shows Sue a path for her continued development and reinforces for you how to increase the capacity of your team. You want to continually be watching for opportunities to move decisions up the tree – have people who are more and more able to make and carry out decisions and less and less need for your direct involvement. This frees you up for being mostly involved in the more critical things that affect the sustainability and growth of the organization."

"That will be great! I work on my priority 1 things and others are effectively doing other important tasks to get results and keep learning. I think I'm ready to have some delegation conversations!"

"Terrific. And as your coach, you know that as a part of our discussion I want you to hear yourself say what you've learned and what you're going to do. So, please walk me through a list of the topics that will be on your agenda in a given delegation conversation."

"Sure. Once I've made a list of possible tasks to delegate, compared that with my capacity matrix, and selected which person to delegate something to and why, I'm ready to have a strategic delegation conversation with that person. I'd start with clarifying the purpose of our conversation in that I have a task to delegate and want to discuss the various expectations and process. I'd tell her about the task and desired organization results and timeline – and if appropriate, what I'm hoping she'll learn from doing the task. I'll share why I chose her – experience, closeness to situation, learning opportunity, and so on. We'll talk about some of the resource needs such as time, money, equipment, people and what she or I will do to ensure those resources are available. We'll also discuss the level of authority for the overall task or specific aspects based on the decision tree model." She paused, then added, "And I'll be sure to explore any questions or concerns she might have about the task and how to get it done. Then we'll close with an agreement on expectations, a statement of commitment from her and encouragement from me, and a plan for when we will next discuss progress."

"Wonderful. And I liked that you added in the pieces of

commitment and encouragement. Anything else on this topic for now?"

"Nope. I think I'm ready to have a few delegation conversations and see how it goes. Thanks, Dad."

"I'll talk to you soon. Love you. Bye."

Chapter 17: ELEVATE

Over the next months, Ariel proudly gave me updates on how well her team was doing. Everyone was focused on their high 5 priorities planned each day as well as their high 5s per quarter. During monthly one-to-ones with each direct report, traffic-light status reports showed mostly green, with an occasional yellow or red. She was particularly pleased that anything that showed yellow or red was turned to green within a few months, meaning that necessary adjustments had been made to get everything on track. She was delegating projects – and authority – to get more important work done, and could see from her capacity matrix that the team was getting stronger across the board.

Further, her quarterly team building activities were paying off. There was a strong sense of collaboration and everyone talked to anyone to keep them abreast of progress or to request help. In their communications, they were all more alert to and leveraging personal styles and communication skills to be sure they understood the what and why of all important conversations. Decisions were made and actions were taken to keep everything moving in the right direction.

Ariel was freed up a bit from daily tasks and was asked to participate more fully in executive team meetings to help with strategic planning. She was also asked to share her capacity planning process, then to help put something in place organization-wide. It was after a recent meeting on capacity planning that she wanted to talk further about another management task.

"Dad, as I've been telling you over the past few months, things are really going well. My team and I have received lots of positive comments on our work results. Many senior managers and peers have commented how my team has strengthened individual and collective knowledge and skills, and our visible focused commitment. With the organization's growth, we've created a new position in another department for someone who will be my peer. I've been asked if I would recommend any of my direct reports for the position. I've got a lot of questions and concerns about that. Any ideas?"

"Ariel, first – congratulations on how well everything is going. Clearly you are using your experience, intuition, and evolving skill set to get terrific results," I acknowledged. "It sounds like we're ready to talk about the next management task that I call 'Elevate'. This employee performance phase happens when a person has consistently performed above the target performance level, has taken on and done well with extra delegated responsibilities, and is ready for a potential promotion. Not everyone who gets to this performance level gets a promotion right away. A lot depends on whether there is an organization need due to a vacancy or newly created position," I explained. "So, what are some of your questions?"

"First, is there some way – one of your 'famous' tools - that helps determine who might be appropriate to promote? Second – assuming there are two or more potential internal candidates, how do we select the best fit? Third – and this one bothers me that I even think of it – if one of my best employees moves to another position, how do I handle the hole that leaves? I'm aware that I'm feeling a little reluctant to let go of someone who helps my team perform so well,"

Ariel admitted. "Those are a few questions to start with. I'm sure I'll have more."

"Great questions. Let's go through them in the order you raised them, although I can hear that the last one may be the most troubling for you."

"Yeah. But now that I said it out loud, I realize how I may feel depends on which person might be elevated. I'm sure the rest of the team and I can cover and a new person can bring some great energy and ideas. More importantly, I think anyone I elevate will likely be highly motivated as we've defined it. She will have an opportunity to bring more value to the organization at the same time she's furthering her own journey toward what's most important to her."

"OK. – some good thoughts. We'll get back to that in a bit. To start – as you expected - I know of a tool that may be useful. This tool is more common in fairly large organizations for identifying people with high potential – sometime called 'HiPos'. It works for any size organization, but may not require the same amount of detail and analysis."

"Sounds good. Let's go through it."

"I assume that the organization has a record of all the most recent performance ratings for all employees. Is that right?"

"Yes – HR has all that information."

"And, from the work you and others have done, do you have a list of the job descriptions and responsibilities for every position?"

"I believe we do, for the most part. I know I have them for all of my people."

"Great. Let's work on just your team. Then, you can share whatever makes sense with the rest of the organization. So, let's create a spreadsheet grid. Some organizations use this for overall succession planning. For now, based on your questions, let's call it 'Potential to Elevate'", I suggested. "Across the top, let's indicate overall knowledge and skills to do the current job. This is a labeling of the position, regardless of the person. Label the axis 'Job Requirements'. Now, based on our previous conversations of employee performance, let's identify some levels of mastery that might be demonstrated in meeting the job requirements."

"Well, if I understand you correctly, I'd say while the employee is in her training phase, her mastery would be pretty low," Ariel suggested.

"Let's call that 'Developmental' and make it the first column. As she moves into Sustaining ...?," I prompted.

"So, she's performing at the target performance level, but there are still things to learn over time. She's not yet fully competent. After a longer time, her knowledge and skills get stronger and she is fully competent to meet the job requirements."

"Then let's break that into two columns. After Developmental, plug in 'Growing Competence' and then 'Fully Competent'. Then, when she is in the gaining phase and you've successfully delegated assignments that are a bit beyond her job, what would you say about her competence to meet the requirements of her current position?"

"Then she'd be at a mastery level. I'll label a fourth column 'Mastery'," Ariel proclaimed.

"Great. So you have four levels of competency that could be described for any position no matter who is in the role."

"Yep. What's next?" she asked, clearly grasping the process.

"Let's create a vertical axis labeled 'Performance Ratings'.

What Does It Mean To Be A Manager?

Use your organization's overall performance rating scale starting with the lowest rating on the bottom row and the highest rating on the top row."

After a moment, Ariel announced, "OK. Here's what I put in. Starting at the bottom and working to the top – 'Does Not Meet Expectations = 0', 'Needs improvement = 1', Meets most but not all expectations = 2', 'Consistently meets all expectations = 3', 'Consistently Exceeds expectations = 4'."

Potential to Elevate

Job requirements	Developmental	Growing Competence	Fully Competent	Mastery
4				
3				
2				
1				
0				

Performance Rating

"So you now have a 5 X 4 grid showing Results compared to Job Requirements."

"Yes. Although, I'd have to say that our practice is that anyone who gets an overall rating of 0 is usually on her way out the door."

"That's fairly typical," I agreed. "Can you now – by memory or reference – fill in the name of each of your employees in one of the boxes?"

"Absolutely. For example, two that we've talked about before are Sue and Mary. For Sue, I'd say she's at a growing competence and she earned a consistently meets. Mary is at Mastery and consistently exceeds."

"As you fill in the rest, you'll start to get an even better sense of where they are. Now with consideration of who is a high-potential performer - a HiPo – ready for promotion, how might you use this grid?"

"Anyone in the upper right – at a mastery level in their current position and consistently exceeding requirements – is ready for promotion!" Ariel declared.

"Absolutely. Some companies extend the potential to

include your upper right 4 boxes. Someone doesn't have to be Superwoman to be eligible for promotion. And again, it will depend on what position is open and who would be the best fit for it."

"So as we fill in this grid, perhaps across the entire organization, we can see who we would suggest is promotable immediately and who needs a bit further development to be ready to elevate. This works well with the capacity matrix and gives me some more ideas on what I might delegate with the intent of preparing someone for promotion."

"Right you are. And, when you look at the potential positions that might open up, you can determine what new or different skills might be needed and plan that into the delegation assignments."

"That will give someone a chance to test drive if they are ready – and if they want – that level of responsibility. This sounds very useful."

"OK. Then let's move on to your next question, which was, 'Assuming there are two or more candidates, how do you determine who is the best fit?'"

"Now that I'm clearer on how we can identify candidates, if two or more are HiPos, then we'd do the same process you and I discussed way back in the Designate task. We would have clarified the position description and requisite knowledge and skills indicating the relative importance of each. Then as we interview candidates, we would put our rankings in the worksheet along with any subjective comments. And, similar to when I interviewed and hired Sue, we need to be sure to talk to each person who is interested and let them know where they stand as we go through the process."

"Great. Now - another question for you. If you become aware of an opportunity that may fit one of your people, what is your role as a manager with respect to letting that person know about it?"

"Well, putting it that way, I guess my responsibility would be to talk with my employee to let her know that I think she is ready for a promotion and might be interested in the opportunity. I would encourage her to consider it, even if one or both of us doesn't want her to leave – at least not yet."

"So, does that bring us to your third question – How do you handle the hole that you'd be left with if you elevate one of your best people?"

What Does It Mean To Be A Manager?

"As I said before, I recognize the right thing to do is help the right person get elevated. I and my team will figure out how to fill any hole that is created."

"And, it may be possible that your elevated employee can help continue with some of the work while in transition. At least, she can help clarify the status of all projects so there is a clean transfer. She may even be able to help interview or train a current or new employee for a bit of time, depending on the requirements of her new position."

"That's a great idea! Whoever is elevated has probably already done some training and coaching with others. She may even have great recommendations on how to spread her work through the team or suggest a specific person to take on her responsibilities. That will certainly ease the transition and sense of loss."

"And, given what you tell me about the levels of teamwork and mutual support, I'm guessing others on the team will see the promotion as a good thing for her and the organization. It's a time for celebration and graduation."

"You're right. I feel better about all of this now."

"OK - and how do you feel about the possibility of one of

your previous direct reports becoming a peer?"

"I'm not a competitive person about that kind of stuff. I'll be proud if that happens and will look forward to further and different conversations."

"And, I think it's a great attribute to have others recognize you as a manager who successfully develops and elevates your employees."

"That would be nice – as long as it's not too many at one time!" Ariel laughed.

"With effective planning, it can work well for everyone. One last question with respect to the Elevate task: Whether the person is promoted to another department or even another level under you, where does that put her in her Employee Development Phases?"

"Oh. I guess it's almost like starting over. Since the position and responsibilities are new for her, she'll be back in a training phase and working to get up to her new target performance level."

"Exactly, and hopefully her new manager will successfully implement all the tasks of management that you've been

What Does It Mean To Be A Manager?

using to help her on her path to further success."

"And I'll do whatever I can to help that manager and whoever is elevated. I realize it won't be my job and I have to be sure I'm not intrusive. But as we become more and more collaborative across the organization, I believe there will be ways I can help in the transition."

"OK. Keep me posted. Good luck determining who might be promotable and the rest of the process. Bye for now."

"Bye, Dad. And thanks again. This was just what I needed."

284

ELIMINATE, REMEDIATE and REINTEGRATE

Chapter 18: ELIMINATE, REMEDIATE and REINTEGRATE

A few weeks later, after catching up on all the personal happenings on both ends, including lots of travel, Ariel asked if I had some time for further exploration of the role of a manager.

"What's up?" I asked as a way of moving right into the conversation.

"Well, first the good news. I did the Potential to Elevate matrix and saw I had two people I thought could be excellent for the new position we discussed. The organization conducted the interviews and used the rating process to make a determination of the best fit. Mary was offered the position and is in transition now while finishing up some of her work and helping me divvy up the rest to others. She's very excited about the opportunity and thoroughly enjoyed the graduation ceremony we did for her."

"Sounds great! Congratulations to you and her," I exclaimed. "You hinted that there was some other news that may not be as good?" I prodded.

"Yes. Unfortunately, I have two employees who have recently been performing consistently below their previous levels in a few areas. I think they are both in Draining and it's taking a lot of my attention and time. And this has all happened since Mary's promotion, so the work load on the team is stressed."

"Do you think that Mary's promotion had anything to do with this change in the other two?"

"Unfortunately, yes. First, Pamela was the other candidate and was not selected. She said she was fine with it at the time, but now I'm not so sure. The other, Ellen, used to work fairly closely with Mary on a couple tasks, and now that Mary's moved on, Ellen is not getting the tasks done correctly or on time, especially a monthly summary report of expenses per client."

"Let's work our way through these situations. We'll start with some general stuff, then get into each of those specific situations. OK?"

"I hope so. I was feeling like a good manager before when everything had been going smoothly. Now I'm wondering if I can handle rough times, especially as I've gotten to know my people better and more deeply. These are my friends, and I'm not sure if I can do what may be needed to fix this," Ariel sighed.

"It's all a part of management. Hopefully, if you do all the other stuff well that we've discussed, you won't have to face this situation very often."

"I hope you're right."

"So, the general comments first. As we've discussed, an employee's performance will typically trend at or slightly above or slightly below the target performance level. Having a specific performance issue may 'simply' be one of those periodic blips below the line. However, if there is a lot of below-the-line performance – and normal participation and coaching haven't had the effect needed, the person may have slipped into Draining."

"Does Draining mean the performance has dropped on all aspects of their performance or possibly only in some areas?" Ariel asked.

"Great question. We don't want to overstate the situation. At present there may be only a few areas of performance that have declined. However, since the coaching you've offered so far hasn't helped the employee get back on track, you are probably noticing – or at least concerned - that the declining performance may spread to other areas of responsibility."

"Yes. That's why I think I may have some draining going on," she sighed.

"When someone's performance shifts into Draining, especially after the kind of engagement you've had with her all along, it may help for you to determine a particular task or set of performance expectations that are leading to the decline – or at least might be the key to helping the employee get back on track. Do you have something in mind for each of them?"

"Definitely. So, if I can help each one figure out ways to

improve a specific key task, then we can possibly leverage that to get back on track across the board."

"It works that way some times. We'll probably revisit this if what you try doesn't work fully. It's also very important to remind yourself that you are trying to help the employee get back on track for success rather than looking for evidence to get rid of her."

"Well I certainly don't want to lose either Ellen or Pamela. So help me think through what I need to do."

"OK. First you need to do a bit of diagnosis."

"What kind of diagnosis?"

"You want to determine what is causing a gap between the employee's performance and your expectations. At a high level, there are two possibilities – a reduction in ability or a reduction in desire. Of course, either one of these may come first, then bring about the other. And, remember, this is no longer one part of the job, you have to address the declining and possibly-spreading trend."

"So, I have to figure out if the reason for draining is due to ability or desire to get the results? How do I do that?"

What Does It Mean To Be A Manager?

"Well, here again, is a great tool. This is a series of questions from *Analyzing Performance Problems* by Robert Mager and Peter Pipe. The first thing they suggest is to be sure there is a gap. You've already done that. Then, ask yourself, 'Is this gap important enough to fix?' I believe you've already done that as well."

"Yes and yes. Although, I can name other situations where the gap wasn't that big and through a little coaching, things got back on track. These situations are different."

"So Mager and Pike suggest the next thing is to determine if the important gap is because the person *can't* do what you're asking or *won't* do it. Their question is, 'If I offered the person a large reward or threatened dire consequences, could that person do what I expect?'"

"You mean like if I offer Ellen $1 million or threaten termination? Well, I guess if Ellen *can't* do it with those kinds of consequences, it's really a question of ability. If she *could* do it, it's a question of desire."

ELIMINATE, REMEDIATE and REINTEGRATE

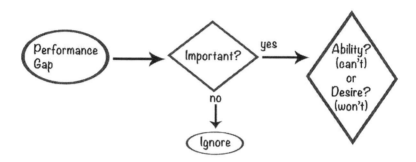

"Right. And depending on which it is, you have different paths to follow for further diagnosis. Let's continue," I suggested. "If it's a lack of ability - that is, the person genuinely cannot do what you're asking, the next question to ask is 'Has it ever been done before correctly – by her or anyone else?'

"And the answer is 'Yes'. Ellen and others – especially Mary - have done it before."

What Does It Mean To Be A Manager?

"If the answer had been 'No' – what do you think would have been the next step?"

"Well, if no one had done it before, we'd have to figure out how to do it and be sure Ellen got appropriate training from scratch. But she has done it before, so where do I go with a 'Yes'?"

"If 'Yes', the next question is 'Does she do it often enough to retain the necessary skills?'"

"That could be a 'No'. She didn't do it that often and I'm not sure if she ever did it without Mary's help. So that would mean retraining or further practice, right?"

"That's right. Or even if the answer is 'Yes', the next question could apply. 'Is there an easier way to do the task?'"

"We're always looking for ways to work smarter. Maybe there is a way some of these things can be simplified. Perhaps we could write out the procedure so even if not done that often, it's very clear how to get the job done."

"That could be good," I agreed. "And finally, you should ask, 'Are there any other obstacles preventing her from doing the task?'"

"I don't think there are – but I get the point. If she didn't have a computer or the software, she couldn't do the task. Since she needs information from other sources, if she wasn't getting cooperation, she couldn't do the task. There's nothing I'm aware of that's keeping her from doing it."

"If there were obstacles, it might be part of your job to help remove them or find work-arounds. This is the management task I call 'Eliminate'."

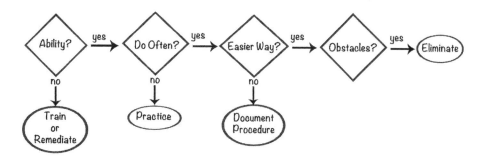

What Does It Mean To Be A Manager?

"Of course. Any further questions from Mager and Pipe?"

"Not on ability. And, it sounds like for Ellen, you think ability might be the cause for the gap. Right?"

"Yes, and I think it's probably that she hasn't been trained sufficiently and done it often enough without Mary for it to stick. We need to write up a procedure and have her go through it a few times so she can get up to speed – assuming she has the ability to do so."

"Great. You've just described a good part of the management task I call 'Remediate'. It includes going through this analysis on the ability side of the question and determining a course of action such as you've described. You could do that on your own – or perhaps even better – in a non-judgmental dialogue with Ellen. After you've stated the gap as you see it, you can use the Mager and Pipe questions to help her get a sense of where the problem and possible solutions might be. It's fine for you to have ideas about potential solutions, but as you know, it's much more powerful if she can come up with ideas and work from there."

"Sounds good. That's what I'll do next with Ellen," she said, sounding more confident. "And if she is able to strengthen her ability on this task, it may give her the confidence to step it up all around or ask for help if needed."

"Exactly."

"Now what about Pamela? She's the one I'm more concerned about because I felt she was gaining, then after not getting the promotion, she's now draining. Before I would have said its 'attitude'. Now I'll say it's desire, because I believe if I offered her $1million or threatened her with termination, she could do the job. She just seems to have lost the spark. She seems burned out."

"Is there a specific task you can focus on where you think it's a question of desire?"

"Sure. Here's one: Talking to clients regarding the specifics of their situation and helping them come up with possible solutions. She used to be terrific at working with clients to get a clear understanding of their options to move forward and make a better situation for themselves. Now, she doesn't dig into the specifics of the situation and just gives generic advice. I think it's making it more difficult for clients to know what steps to take and feel the ownership to move forward." Ariel sighed. "And that's the mission of our work!"

"Sounds tough. Mager and Pipe's first question on the

desire side is, 'Has she been given feedback to let her know that you perceive a gap?'"

"At first, no. I thought she was just going through a little funk after she didn't get the promotion, so I gave her some space. When she seemed not to improve, I did talk with her. I thought she heard me and re-committed, but it hasn't stuck."

"Mager and Pipe's next question – 'Is the desired behavior punishing?' That is, will doing it be more 'painful' than not doing it?"

"No. I wouldn't think so. It used to be what really got her juices flowing. Now, she seems to have lost her mojo."

"Well, Mager and Pipe suggest that if it did feel punishing, you should look for ways to reduce the punishing aspects, or at least add more positive consequences to help balance things out. So, the next question is 'Is the undesired behavior being positively reinforced?' Is she feeling some reward for not doing the task as expected?"

"Again, I don't think so. Perhaps there might have been a passive aggressive kind of thinking – like 'I'll show them they can't overlook me'. Then she might have felt rewarded for getting away with something. But that wouldn't be the

Pamela I've known and respected."

"Mager and Pipe's recommendation would have been to reduce the positives or balance with negative consequences. So, if it's not that, 'Does performance – positive or negative – matter? And to whom?'"

"That's my leverage!" Ariel exclaimed excitedly. "It does matter to her – or at least it used to. She took a lot of pride in her work and the positive difference it made in clients' lives. She was definitely on mission and it seemed to give her personal joy."

"You may have identified the problem and be on the road for a potential solution. But Mager and Pipe ask one more question – the same as on the ability side. 'Are there any obstacles preventing her from doing the task?'"

"Not that I'm aware of and would need to eliminate. I'll need to explore that with her."

What Does It Mean To Be A Manager?

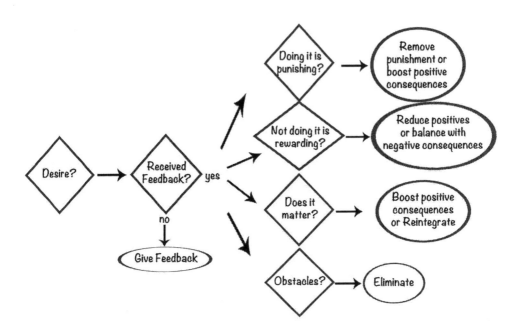

"Well, we've just gone through another management task. I call this one 'Reintegrate'. Through these questions and further discussions, you want to help her get back in touch with her reason for doing this work. Get back to the journey she shares – for a time – with the organization; where how she does her job matters to her, to the client, and to the organization."

"Well, this discussion has given me a sense of the next steps on my journey with her. And, as with Ellen, I want to help her walk through these questions and see what she discovers and recommends. I hope she will see the potential for reintegration and fully embrace it. I'll let you know what happens. Thanks, Dad."

"You're welcome, and good luck."

What Does It Mean To Be A Manager?

Chapter 19: MIGRATE

Another two weeks passed and I was anxious to hear how Ariel was doing with Ellen and Pamela. I sent her a quick text and asked if she had time to give me an update. She responded shortly and said there was much to talk about. We agreed on a time that would work later that day.

"So, what's the story?" I asked. "I've been thinking about you a lot since we last spoke and hoping you were doing OK."

"Well, for the most part I am. I met with Ellen right after we spoke and we had a great conversation. She acknowledged that most of the expense reporting had been handled by Mary. That even though she was trained how to do it, each time it came due, Mary just offered to get it done because she'd be faster at it. Then Ellen suggested that if she were re-trained and had to do it each month, she thought she could handle it. She suggested that she could do it more frequently, like a mid-month report, to keep her skills up. But we agreed that would just be adding workload that might not be necessary. She loved the idea of writing down the procedure and then suggested she could create some wizards and templates that would make things go even faster. She was really pumped to give it a go. Now she's coming to me with other ideas on how to improve other parts of her job. Even though I didn't think desire was a part of the reason for the gap, she sure has picked up energy and focus. She's back in Sustaining I think."

"Ariel, that's wonderful! Great job! And, how about Pamela?"

"A bit of a different story. The short version is that we had a great discussion and she has regained her desire to do the task we discussed. And it's going well – the old Pamela is back. The downside is that she shared with me that her disappointment in not getting the promotion made her really think hard about what she's doing and if that is the path she wants to be on. She acknowledged that though disappointed, she was also somewhat relieved because she realized she didn't want the extra travel and additional time commitment to do the job that Mary now has. And at the same time, partly because I encouraged her and suggested she was ready for a promotion, she began thinking about what else she could do with her knowledge and skill set that would pay her well and not involve travel and time."

"So now you're wondering if she can maintain the improvements and for how long?"

"I don't want to lose Pamela – and I want her to be happy and continue growing. I just don't know if I have an appropriate opportunity for her in my department in the foreseeable future."

"Have you considered – or discussed – other possibilities to keep her fully reintegrated and motivated in her current position?"

"We did explore some further things I could delegate that would give her more responsibilities, challenge and variety. We also discussed the reality that unless she took my job or some other management position opened up as it had for

---

Mary, that there probably wouldn't be much we could do with respect to compensation, travel expectations, and time commitments."

"Some organizations find that challenge, variety and responsibility do keep people engaged longer, even without the additional compensation. Regarding travel and time, some organizations are finding ways to use technology to cut down on travel time – and expense. Any ideas from that?"

"As an organization, we're considering remote work and travel reduction. Given the nature of her job, I don't see a lot of leverage there. Her work entails a lot of face-to-face with our clients."

"Well, I don't want to push it because things may change and she'll be fully integrated back into her current role. However, this is a good time to introduce the task of management I call 'Migrate'. Let's assume you have an employee who is showing signs of burnout or disconnect, and you've clarified that she's wanting something different in her work experience. It may be time to consider if there is another position on your team or elsewhere in the organization that might be a better fit."

"We're not a large organization and there probably aren't

many options."

"It may not work out. But since she's a good employee and engaged with the mission, it's possible there could be something that exists or could be created."

"Actually, I was approached by a fellow manager – Michael - about his situation a few months ago. He told me about one of his employees that he was looking to transfer – or as you say, migrate. Michael said she had been a stellar performer before and thought the work we do is similar and that the culture I created in my department might be more suitable to getting her back on track."

"And?" I prompted.

"I felt bad for him and his situation, but I didn't feel I had a place for her. Also, organization policy makes it very difficult to do an internal transfer when someone is on a performance improvement plan."

"Why do you think that is?"

"I think the organization wants to help people be successful in place. Years ago - and well before my time – there had been a lot of people moving around and it got a codename of

'Dump or Jump'. Some people felt that some managers who were ineffective in helping employees be successful would just 'Dump' them into another department and wash their hands, so to speak. There was also a sense of a few employees who were overly-focused on their own career or compensation and would seek out other positions to 'jump' to trying to get ahead. Although some internal transfers worked out well, there were too many that didn't, and the organization was significantly less effective in helping our clients. That led to some of the policies we have now about required length of time in one position before consideration of a transfer, the employee needs to have a clean and positive record of results and culture fit – no transfer if in the progressive discipline process, and in some cases, only lateral compensation for lateral moves at least for six months."

"Sounds like the organization may have had a painful lesson. I have lots of assumptions around what you've said, but let's get back to Pamela," I suggested. "I hear you saying that there are some organizational norms and policies that may make a migration more difficult, especially if there is not currently an open position that would benefit from her expertise. Do you have an important need for a special project in your department that could be an appropriate assignment?"

"Nothing that we're not already doing. She's in charge of one of those and it's helping her motivation. And she doesn't have extra time or bandwidth. Also there is no budget for anything else right now."

"Well, I agree you don't necessarily want to create something new just for her. However, if there were something that was a Priority 1 opportunity that could replace something on her plate, that might be a reason to reconsider."

"If that were the case, I'd be all over it. We're continually re-assessing our priorities and there doesn't seem to be anything else calling out loud enough to make a switch. And I believe if we did make a switch, I could easily delegate lower-priority tasks to others and change her focus. So, I don't think that's holding us back."

"So it feels like there's nothing you can do. That might be OK and she'll stay on for a while doing good work. Or, she may decide to pursue something else."

"I don't want to lose her, but I've thought about it– and talked with her and others. There doesn't seem to be anything else right now. I guess we'll just have to take that risk and deal with the situation if and when it changes," she said matter-of-factly.

MIGRATE

"Sometimes, when I feel I'm at the end of my options, I move in a very different direction. So, one more possibility you might consider. I've been involved in a few organizations where they wanted to grow and retain good employees, but had no suitable internal situation that would work. They were able to figure out how to reduce the internal work load – possibly including travel – by shifting someone to part-time and 'loaning' the expertise to a partner organization or the community for a period of time. Sometimes, it was a trade and someone from another organization came in to fill in on the work. In each of those scenarios, things worked well for the 'loaned' employee and both organizations."

"That's an interesting idea I hadn't heard of. Tell me a bit more."

"In one case, an employee in the finance department of a telecommunications company was loaned to a non-profit in health care to help clean up the accounting practices. The telecom company paid his entire wages and benefits for a year and was able to claim an in-kind contribution for tax purposes. He got to put in practice some of what he'd learned on the job and in his MBA program. After 1 year, he returned full time to the telecom company with a promotion into management."

What Does It Mean To Be A Manager?

"And the other?" Ariel asked eagerly.

"A woman executive at a bank with lots of management expertise and community connections was loaned half time to a non profit. The bank paid her full salary for a year. At the end of the year, all parties agreed that she should move to a full-time management position in the non-profit. Given her life circumstances and her passion for the mission of the organization, she agreed to a fairly substantial decrease in compensation that the non-profit could afford. It's been a terrific migration adding value to the organization and more significance to her life."

"Great stories, Dad. I want to think about that some more and talk with others and Pamela about it. There might be some significant questions regarding budget and her compensation, but not necessarily undoable. I have lots of ideas popping in my head about some possibilities," Ariel exclaimed excitedly.

"Clearly that pushed some buttons. I leave you to think on it," I offered. Then added, "With the migrate task – there may be a long-term or permanent transfer. Or – like the migration of birds – she may go away for a while and come back rejuvenated and ready for another season."

"And, there may not be an appropriate opportunity, so she may chose to leave voluntarily. I've been afraid of that. This gives me one more avenue to explore. Thanks, Dad."

"Well, keep in mind – as you did when Mary was promoted – whether she migrates or voluntarily separates, have her help you and the organization through the transition. Some organizations offer a time-limited contract with additional compensation to assist in smoothing the way. If it comes to that - she sounds like the kind of person who embraces the mission and would want the organization to be successful if and when she departs her current position."

"I certainly hope so. I'll keep you posted."

"Good luck. Talk with you soon. "

"Love you, Dad."

Chapter 20: TERMINATE

The text message came in with a smiley face and a few times open for another phone conversation. It had been just over two weeks since we'd talked about Pamela and I assumed it would be good news. I immediately texted back and selected one of her available times and asked her to initiate the call so I wouldn't disturb her if she wasn't quite ready.

"Dad! Great news! When Pamela and I got to talking about how to keep her engaged and the improbability of an internal transfer, she shared that she had anticipated that, so had started looking for another opportunity. She said she was in no rush, but something had come up quickly that excited her. She shared that she was really torn because she is dedicated to our mission, her work is very important to her, and she enjoys working with me and the rest of the team. On the other hand, the travel and other time requirements – especially needing to be on call – was wearing on her more and more. Then she told me about the other opportunity and asked my advice." Ariel paused.

"And then what?" I jumped in unable to contain myself.

"Well, the position she got excited about was under a grant and would only be the equivalent of two days a week. No travel. No on-call requirements. Close to where she lives. It would pay well, but wouldn't be enough by itself. We explored if there was a way for us to keep her for three days a week and made sure there would be no conflicts of interest. We just finished getting all the details worked out and it gets put in place in two weeks to allow us time to transition the rest of her work to others on the team. We are so excited. It looks like a win-win all the way around!"

"Ariel, that sounds like an elegant solution. Congratulations to everyone."

What Does It Mean To Be A Manager?

"Well, Dad. Thanks again to you for your support and planting a seed that grew a little differently. And also, thanks for many of our previous conversations. Pamela and I used the priority matrix to help us plan what she would do and what we would delegate. We used the capacity matrix to determine who had the knowledge and skills to take over some of her tasks immediately or needed to develop those skills. We used the Delegation Planning Tool to look at all the potential delegates inside and outside the organization and have come up with a very workable plan. I do think I will likely need to hire another staff member soon, but I can see bringing in someone more at an entry level and developing him or her over time. That will help us manage the budget given Pamela's continued but reduced compensation."

"Well done. Clearly you have been utilizing your growing knowledge and skills as a manager to develop and retain excellent employees. You're continually building the strength of your team and of the entire organization so you are even better able to assist your clients. I'm proud of you, Ariel."

"Thanks again. I appreciate that. I've been hearing similar compliments from my bosses and peers." She paused, and in a quieter tone, "In fact, it was a call from one of my peers that I wanted to talk to you about as well."

TERMINATE

"Hum. Sounds interesting. What's up?"

"You remember me mentioning Michael, my peer with the employee he was thinking about transferring?"

"Uh huh."

"Well, he asked me to join him for a cup of coffee this morning. Turns out his employee, Rebecca, is still struggling. He thinks it may be time to let her go and asked me if I had any ideas. I said I had never had to fire someone, but that I'd ask you about it and get back to him shortly. Any help?"

"Wow. Sorry to hear it seems to have come to that. You have been fortunate not to have had the experience. My guess is, if you continue to be a manager or higher, you will be faced with that as well. It's not easy to let someone go, even when there are justifiable reasons," I acknowledged. "So – first a few comments. Before it is appropriate to 'Terminate' – the name of this management task – there are a number of things to consider. I can't tell you the specifics for his situation, but I can walk you through some considerations."

"OK. What's first?"

What Does It Mean To Be A Manager?

"Does your organization have an employee handbook or similar document that lays out the mutual expectations and agreements related to working for the company?"

"Yes we do. And it includes performance expectations, behavior expectations according to our values, and requires adherence to policies. Each employee was supposed to read the handbook when they started with the organization and then sign a document saying she had read it and agree to abide by it."

"Good. Second, does the handbook specify by some name, a progressive discipline policy?"

"Yes, and we call it that. And when I came in as a manager, I received further training on it as well. Generally, we have four levels for most performance related issues, which is what Michael's dealing with. Assuming there has been feedback and coaching like you and I have discussed, the first level of progressive disciple is a verbal warning. We have to be sure to say something to the employee so it's clear that this is now more serious than the coaching we've been doing. Also, that the manager will document the verbal warning, but keep it in the manager's file for now. If there is a need for the next level, the verbal warning document will accompany a formal written warning into the personnel file."

"So far, pretty typical."

"It's usually at this point that the manager and employee – sometimes with help from HR – will document what we call a PIP – Performance Improvement Plan. That specifies behaviors and results that need to be demonstrated for a minimum of 90 days. Any infraction can lead to further disciplinary action up to and including termination. The manager and employee both sign it and it goes into the personnel file."

"Again pretty typical. I have seen some organizations that may wait til a second written warning before a documented improvement plan."

"Our third level – and it's optional – is to put the person on suspension for a limited time to encourage them to decide if they want to and are able to improve. It's a last chance. Sometimes the employee is paid; other times not. Reasons for each are explained in the manual."

"To your knowledge, has anyone come back from a suspension and got back on track?"

"Yes. I've heard of a couple examples. Those employees saw the light and were able to get things turned around over time with the help of their manager. But usually, no. Some have taken the time to think it through and either said good-bye or said they wanted to improve, and were not able to do so."

"And your fourth level?"

"That is termination. It could be immediate or allowed to take place over a little time depending on the circumstances. Again, these steps are for performance and some behavior-related issues. If there is a more serious behavior – such as breech of confidence, creating a threatening environment – I think they call it 'hostile and intimidating' – drug abuse, and so on, that can be grounds for immediate termination. If necessary, there may be a short suspension to allow for an internal investigation."

"Sounds like you're really aware of your organization's policies. Do you think Michael is as well?"

"Absolutely. He shared the entire progressive discipline history they've gone through with Rebecca. She had gone all the way through a suspension and said she wanted to keep her job and would try harder. She has not been successful and it's been taking an inordinate amount of Michael's time and focus to supervise her. That's why he's decided it's time to terminate her."

"OK – a few other general things. In addition to following your own organization's policies – to be fair and consistent – Michael needs to understand whatever laws or regulations exist at the federal, state, or local level that might have an impact."

"Yes. We talked about some of that as well. We are an at-will state, so essentially we can terminate someone at any time without specific cause. That is also spelled out in the employee handbook that everyone signs. We also recognize that we need to follow legal guidelines with respect to potential discrimination, harassment, and retaliation. We're supposed to work with HR and possibly our lawyers to be sure we are doing any termination appropriately according to our policies and any laws."

"Right. And it sounds like you're both aware of the next general thing I was going to mention which is to be sure to engage the assistance of HR and your legal advisors."

"Yep. Got it."

"OK. It seems that brings us to how to conduct the actual termination meeting. Is that what you wanted ideas on to help Michael?"

"Sort of. He's been working with HR. He's got a script of what to say and what not to say. He's been told to be brief and concise. Be clear that this is a termination and not another chance. He's not to promise anything like helping her find another job, being a reference, or staying in touch. He is to meet with her with HR present and in a neutral location, then leave and let HR take over with the details of getting her organization-owned materials, passwords, keys, and walk her through the next steps for collecting her personal belongings and signing up for any temporary continuation of benefits," she said. "All the stuff I just said sounds so rational and straightforward – and uncaring. What he told me is that he's not sure how to handle the emotional side."

"So he's got the structure and the process. He's looking for the human side."

"That's it."

"Well I don't know Rebecca – or for that matter, Michael – so it's hard to anticipate what might show up for either of them. So let's you and I walk through some possibilities you can help him think through and prepare for. Since you've never been fired or fired someone," I suggested, "name a few situations in which you – or someone you knew – experienced a significant loss."

"I've thought about this a lot since he asked and I'm drawing from a lot of different experiences. I remember a friend telling me she'd failed a class needed for graduation, and another person I knew had a bad accident and totaled his car. And I'm remember how I felt when grandma passed."

"That's a broad range and I'm sure it will help you tap into some of the possible emotions. So, back to Rebecca. What do you guess might be a reaction she could have to the news that she is being terminated?"

"I think one reaction might be shock. Despite all the conversations and even the suspension, she may feel very surprised."

"And how might that show up?"

"Denial. She might not believe this is happening. Or she might be stunned and just sit silently."

"And a possible response from Michael?" I prompted.

What Does It Mean To Be A Manager?

"First, allow the message to sink in. Don't try to jump in to save her." After a pause, "Especially if Rebecca just sits there in silence. Give her a few moments. Maybe offer to repeat the message if she didn't actually seem to hear it, but don't pound it in."

"What else might Michael do if she's in denial?"

"Well if she's in denial, I could imagine her apologizing and say it won't happen again. She might try to bargain. So, Michael has to make sure she understands this is a termination and not another chance. He could remind her of previous conversations and warnings."

"Usually in the initial script, Michael would likely have referred to those previous conversations and how that has led to the decision to terminate. Again, he doesn't want to beat her up or get into a debate or negotiation at this point. The decision has been made."

"Michael also mentioned that in previous conversations Rebecca had felt she was being singled out and started to point out behaviors of other people. I remember talking with Michael before about how he's got to remind her that this is about her performance and not that of others. At the same time, he made a note about that tactic and commented in his private notes about looking into her allegations to be sure he was being fair."

"What other reaction might she have?"

"Crying. That would be really tough for Michael – or me, too, for that matter."

"That can be a tough one. And sometimes it can be faked as a bargaining tool. Assume it's genuine, how would you suggest Michael respond?"

"I suggest he just stay quiet and give her a few moments to compose herself. Perhaps offer a tissue or glass of water. And if she seems like she needs a little more time, he and HR could offer to leave the room for a few minutes. That's why it would be good to be in a neutral location so they can leave rather than her having to go out and be seen by anyone else."

"Good thinking. And after she's composed herself?"

"He's got to get back on script to make sure he and HR cover everything they need to."

"OK. Any other reaction you can think of?"

What Does It Mean To Be A Manager?

"Well, the one that concerns me most is if the other person gets angry – starts yelling, gets threatening, or even becomes physical."

"That can be very worrisome. How would you suggest Michael handle that possible reaction?"

"That's where I'm sure he'd be glad there's another person in the room! Also, I guess he could let her vent a bit. Or – like with some of the others we talked about – he could give her some time or space to recompose herself. I'd make sure there's nothing in the room she could start throwing around," she laughed uncomfortably.

"That's a very good suggestion. If he anticipated strong anger as a possible reaction based on how he knows her, he should choose the location and environment to ensure mutual safety. Sometimes, Security is alerted ahead of time and is standing by if needed. On one occasion I was involved in a long time ago, we ended up calling the police to help escort the person out of the building and see that he got home safely without causing any injury."

"Wow! Did that really happen?!"

"It did. I was not the direct manager, but was asked to assist because of my physical size and position in the company. We had anticipated a strong reaction and had asked the employee to wait til after normal business hours to have a conversation. We surreptitiously had other employees leave by 5 pm." Then, after sensing Ariel's reaction, I added, "Please remember that this kind of emotional outburst is extremely rare. In fact, if the entire disciplinary process is handled appropriately, the actual termination conversation should not be a surprise. Even so, because of its finality, it can bring up a variety of emotional responses."

"I get it. Here's one other thing that I had thought about. I remember a time during some of my training on empathetic listening, when a young woman was sharing her feelings, a young man said something like 'I know how you must feel'. Then the woman got angry saying he couldn't possibly know how *she* felt, because he wasn't her. Then he tried to tell her 'Things will be okay' and she was angry at him again. So, I will warn Michael to be careful not to overly empathize and not to try to minimize Rebecca's feelings. Even though he is a great empathetic listener, that is not his role in this conversation."

"Some of that may depend on his relationship with Rebecca and what role and skill the HR person has in the process. Generally, I think you've identified the most common reactions and ways to respond. Do you think this is what Michael was hoping you could help him with?"

"Exactly. I'll probably walk him through some of this the same way you did with me. If he can anticipate what's most likely to show up, he and HR can be better prepared to handle it. Thanks, Dad."

"You're welcome. Wish him well from me, too."

"I will. And I'll let you know what I hear about how it went."

"OK. Bye. Love you. And again, congratulations to you and Pamela."

"Thanks. Love you, too. Bye."

RUMINATE

Chapter 21: RUMINATE

A few weeks later, we were completing our family Skype call with Ariel. She filled us in on so many exciting things happening in her life: her deepening and evolving relationship with her boyfriend, some non-work travel around the state, some of her many craft and musical activities in the community, her volunteer youth work. It seems everyone in our family makes time to do their job fully and also to be engaged in a variety of other activities that provide meaningful ways to develop multiple aspects of ourselves while often giving back to our chosen communities.

What Does It Mean To Be A Manager?

As we were ending the call and everyone saying their goodbyes, Ariel asked me for a few more minutes so she could update me on what had happened since our last coaching conversation.

"I know you wanted to hear how things went with Michael and the termination of Rebecca. Long story short, after our conversation he felt much more prepared and did some further planning with HR. At the actual termination meeting, Rebecca did seem to be surprised and said she thought she was getting better. She tried to bargain and make promises to improve. Having anticipated that, Michael was able to clarify that there were no more chances. That she was being terminated. Then she started to cry. She apologized that she'd been a 'bad employee' and was fearful about what she would do now that she'd lost her job – and the income that her family depended on. Michael admitted to me later how heart wrenching that was for him and how he wanted to help her, that she is not a bad person, and tell her things would be OK. Fortunately, instead, he gave her some tissues and time, and she composed herself. Michael was able to complete his portion and left the next steps to HR."

"Sounds like it was hard and that he handled it well. I'm glad to hear that. I wouldn't want terminating people to become cavalier."

"The other thing he told me is how he went around and talked to the rest of his employees and other people she worked with to let them know she would no longer be working at the organization. He was careful not to get into reasons and the process. However, he was taken aback by how many of the people he talked to shared comments like 'I'm not surprised' or 'What took you so long?' When he and I talked after that, we both acknowledged that sometimes we may stick longer with someone – at work or outside of work – hoping that things will change. More to think about."

"It sounds like you were talking about the three sisters that often show up in relationships – Faith, Hope, and Charity. At the beginning and perhaps for a long time, we have faith that someone will do well. As the person or relationship starts to slip for whatever reason, we have hope that things will somehow improve. Then as things slip further, charity comes into the picture. We continue to provide money, time, and energy out of our good intentions."

"Yes, and although it's really hard for me to think this way, sometimes the best – or right – thing to do is put an end to the charity, because only then will the other person be able to move on. Me, too, for that matter."

"It's often a fine line between charity and enabling."

What Does It Mean To Be A Manager?

"Well, on the positive side – and going back over many of our conversations over the last several months, Sue is continuing to be sustaining at or mostly above her target performance level. Ellen has definitely returned to hers and is very much re-engaged. After helping plan for some transitions, Pamela is moving to part-time with us next week while starting her new other part-time job. We've started interviewing for a new entry-level person to take on some of Pamela's work and have lined up a training plan to get the new person enculturated, motivated, and educated efficiently. And we're addressing our most important priorities, achieving great results on time and within budget."

"And how's Mary doing in her new role?"

"Oh yes. She moved quickly from Gaining when she was on my team to Training in her new management role. She's definitely coming up to speed and says she has more to learn. She and I also talked about Ellen's struggles and Mary's well-intentioned part in that situation. She recognizes more than ever that she needs to train people to do their tasks without her taking over. She's also starting to use the capacity matrix and the delegation planning tools to help her more effectively clarify her team's priorities and develop knowledge and skills across the board."

RUMINATE

"Ariel, you've done a wonderful job on all 18 Tasks of Management that support success throughout the 5 Phases of Employee Performance. Congratulations!"

"Thanks. But wait a minute. I have only 17 Tasks in my notes. Did we miss something?"

"No. It's something you've clearly been doing all along. I call that task, 'Ruminate'. You have continued to step back from the day-to-day situations and think through what you've learned and how to be an even more effective manager. That shows up in how you've shared ideas and tools with your colleagues and continually referred back to various tasks and how to apply them in new situations."

"Well some things – if you'll pardon the pun – do keep coming up and need to be chewed on and re-digested."

"Oh Ariel – I'm moooved by your insights!"

"OK. So now that we've gone over the 5 Phases and the 18 Tasks, I do feel I understand some of what it means to be a manager a whole lot better than I did when I started. I know there will be many other questions as specific things come up. Our management team is already talking about the up-coming budget cycle, cross-departmental teamwork, how to

---

build a best-in-class workplace, how to have more effective meetings, and challenges of multi-generational and an extremely diverse workplace and client base."

"I'm here if and when you want to talk," I offered.

"Thanks much," Ariel said with genuine appreciation. "Now, Dad, what does it mean to be a leader?"

Ariel's Binder

What Does It Mean To Be A Manager?

There are five Performance Phases related to any employee's PERFORMANCE over TIME. Some things happen before the employee begins the job. Most employees will experience at least two of the phases for any position they are in. There are 18 Tasks of Management that correlate to the performance phases.

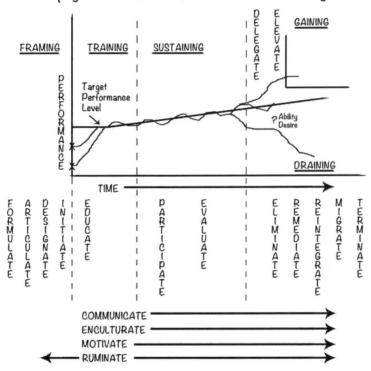

Employee Performance Phases and 18 Tasks of Management

FRAMING – The work done prior to an employee starting the job that defines the job, Target Performance Level, and talent acquisition.

TRAINING – The work over time done to enable an employee, no matter the initial level of skills and knowledge, to move up the learning curve to the Target Performance Level.

SUSTAINING – The ongoing performance at, slightly above, or slightly below the Target Performance Level over time. Note – the Target Performance Level typically rises over time. This phase could continue indefinitely.

GAINING – When an employee continually and consistently performs at or above the Target Performance Level, additional responsibilities are assigned while in the same job. In some cases, an employee may be promoted to another position with additional responsibilities. Note – such a promotion restarts the Performance Phases.

DRAINING – If an employee continually and consistently performs below the Target Performance Level, there has been a decrease in ability and/or desire to do the job. Work must be done to enable the employee to return to the Target Performance Level or to move on from the job.

What Does It Mean To Be A Manager?

FORMULATE – Determine organization, division, department, and team goals; Determine the need for a specific job

ARTICULATE – Discuss the goals with various stakeholders and define the SMART goals for the specific job; define the Target Performance Level required to achieve those goals.

SMART Goals

Specific

Measureable

Achievable

Relevant

Time-bound

DESIGNATE – Recruit, interview, and hire/promote someone to do the specific job

Comparing Candidates									
Position:									
		Candidate A		Candidate B		Candidate C		Candidate D	
Skills, Knowledge and Values	Weight (1)	Average rate (2)	weight x rate	Average rate (2)	weight x rate	Average rate (2)	weight x rate	Average rate (2)	weight x rate
Skill 1									
Skill 2									
Skill 3									
...									
Knowledge 1									
Knowledge 2									
Knowledge 3									
...									
Value 1									
Value 2									
Value 3									
...									
Total									

(1) Weight – must have day 1 = 5, must have in 3 months = 4, nice to have 3, 2, or 1
(2) Average from all interviewers

What Does It Mean To Be A Manager?

INITIATE – Onboard the new/promoted employee and mutually agree on activities to deepen the connection to the job, co-workers, and organization

12 possible categories of action for on-boarding an employee

1. Position
2. Projects
3. Process
4. People
5. Partner(s)
6. Place
7. Provisions
8. Paperwork
9. Power
10. Publicity
11. Past, Present and Potential
12. Probation

COMMUNICATE – Starts with the interviewing process and continues throughout the Performance Phases – Use skills and content to ensure mutual understanding of what is important and why; provide effective feedback and ongoing coaching

Ladder of Inference

from Chris Argyris & "The Fifth Discipline" by Peter Senge

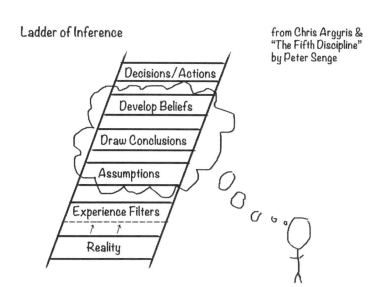

What Does It Mean To Be A Manager?

Slow down

Meta-conversation

Purpose - why we're talking about what
Process - how we'll share thoughts, facts, opinions, beliefs
techniques - conversation, structured dialog, brainstorming, groups
Payoff - result/outcome leading to any next steps of who, what, by when

Listening
Already Listening
Paraphrase
Emotional Intelligence

Conflict
Different Dictionaries

Thomas-Kilmann Conflict Modes

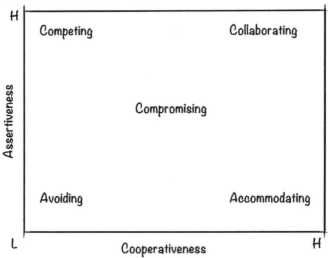

from Kenneth Thomas
& Ralph Kilmann

ENCULTURATE – Starts with the interviewing process and continues throughout the Performance Phases – conversations and activities to create and build the desired culture

Nine Building Blocks of Trust

Relationship Trust

Reciprocity = Integrity: wholeness, unification, indivisible
Have my back even when I'm not present
Common Goals and Expectations to make the right stuff happen
Shared Values: Agreement on what's most important and why
Commonalities and Mutual Respect: Shared experiences, cooperative efforts, proximity, personality, gender, ethnicity, language, culture
Consistency and Predictability: Talks the Talk. Walks the Walk.

Transactional Trust

Ability to Produce Results: Has the knowledge and skills needed.
Positive Intention: Means well. Wants to do the right thing.
Honesty: Tells me the truth. Doesn't lie.

What Does It Mean To Be A Manager?

MOTIVATE – Starts with the interviewing process and continues throughout the Performance Phases – conversations and activities that help an employee feel a connection between their personal sense of purpose and significance and the work they are asked to perform

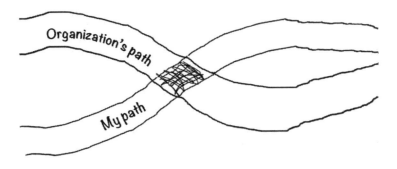

5 Whys

Ask questions to help dig deeper
Stay neutral; no judgment
What's important to you in your life that working here helps you do, have, or be?

Motivation questions:
What do you want to do?
What do you want to have?
Who do you want to be?

Probe deeper –
Why is that important to you?
How would doing/having/being that make you feel?
If you do/have/be that, what would that mean to you?

What is important to you in your life that working here helps you do, have, or be?

Remember – it's about choice!

Motivation Hierarchy

What Does It Mean To Be A Manager?

EDUCATE – conversations and activities that develop the knowledge and skills to deliver results at the Target Performance Level

Positive Reinforcement – 3 parts in any order:

What specific results were achieved

Who benefitted from the achievement

What behavior or characteristic enabled the achievement

Corrective feedback and coaching

1. Assume good intentions
2. Focus on the behavior, not the person
3. Request change including reasons behind the request
4. Invite the person to share their perspective of what happened and why
5. Clarify and confirm each other's understanding of what happened
6. Brainstorm ideas for positive change
7. Finalize who will do what by when – and possibly why
8. Gain commitment for performance
9. Follow up

PARTICIPATE – ongoing conversations and activities that provide reinforcement for good work and coaching for improvements; ongoing performance management matched with a variety of situations; team building for strong collaboration; priority and time management

Traffic light check in for SMART goals

Green = on track to achieve goal as planned
Yellow = a bit behind but know what to do to get back on track
Red = behind and at risk of not achieving goal or not sure what to do

- If green, ask for example(s) of person's success.
- If yellow, ask what happened that got person behind and what ideas/plan to get back on track.
- If red, ask what happened that got person behind and what help they need from who to get back on track.

Adaptation from Blanchard "Situational Leadership"

Low Ability + High Desire -> training and frequent feedback

Medium Ability + High Desire -> coaching with less frequent feedback, often self-assessment

High Ability + High Desire -> empowerment; agree on results and timelines; employee asks for help when needed

What Does It Mean To Be A Manager?

Regular one-to-one potential agenda

Remember tasks of enculturation, motivation, and communication
• Status on goals and projects – use traffic light
• Work relationships
• Career direction
• Life in general

ABCs
  Antecedents
  Behaviors
  Consequences – perceived as positive, negative, neutral, or non-existent

Perceived as	Next likely behavior
Positive	- Repeat same
	- Do even more of same
Negative	- Stop
	- Do even more of same for reward of attention
Neutral or non-existent	- Continue same
	- Do more of same for reward of attention
	- Stop

Further considerations of consequences:
  Certainty
  Immediacy
  Frequency
  Strength

Johari Window - from Joseph Lutt & Harrington Ingham

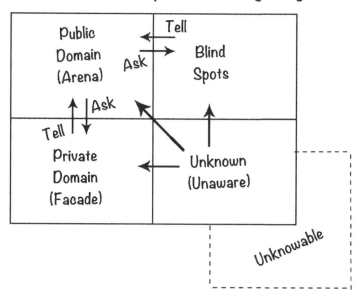

What Does It Mean To Be A Manager?

EVALUATE – formal performance assessment to review what was achieved and how it was achieved relative to the SMART goals and cultural values

Performance Evaluation – No Surprises!

Priority Matrix

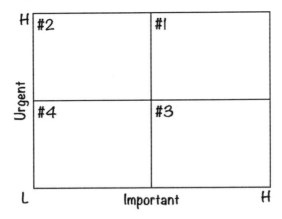

DELEGATE – provide relevant opportunities for further variety, challenge, responsibility and significance; what to delegate to whom, why, when and how; protocols for decision making and accountability

Delegation Possibilities					
Possible Tasks	Organizational Priority	Special Skills and Knowledge (1)	Who could do this? (2)	Readiness (3)	Why (4)
...					

(1) See codes for special skills and knowledge

(2) Names of my employees, other employees, peers, boss, clients, suppliers, consultants

(3) Readiness: Now = N, With training = T

(4) Why: Development = D, Team Capacity = T, Close to Situation = C, Experienced with kind of task = E, Potential Partnership = P, Available = A

What Does It Mean To Be A Manager?

Capacity Matrix		Sue		Mary		Ellen		Pamela		Dan	
Skills and Knowledge	Code	Now	6 mo	Now	6 mo	Now	6 mo	Now	6 mo	Now	6 mo
Use Excel template to track client meetings	E-TC	M	H	H	H						
Create Excel spreadsheets	E-CS	L	M	H	H						
Create Excel Templates	E-CT	L	L	H	H						
...											

Decision Tree – from Susan Scott, Fierce Conversations

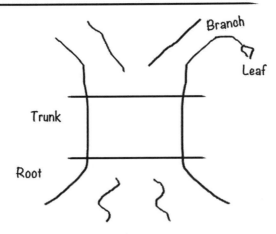

348

Ariel's Binder

ELEVATE – the decision and process to promote an employee; succession planning; career development

Potential to Elevate

Job requirements	Developmental	Growing Competence	Fully Competent	Mastery
4				
3				
2				
1				
0				

Performance Rating

What Does It Mean To Be A Manager?

From Robert Mager & Peter Pipe, Analyzing Performance Problems

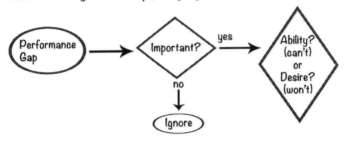

ELIMINATE –diagnose performance issues; implement progressive discipline; identify and work to remove or lessen barriers to performance

REMEDIATE – provide re-training or refreshment to ensure the knowledge and skills are sufficient to do the job

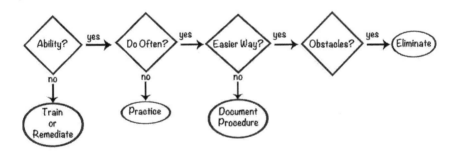

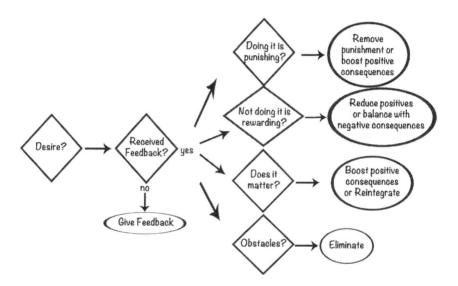

REINTEGRATE – help an employee reconnect their sense of purpose to the job requirements

What Does It Mean To Be A Manager?

Progressive Discipline – follow the organization's guidelines

- Corrective feedback and coaching
- Verbal warning(s)
- Written warning(s)
- Suspension
- Probation
- Termination

MIGRATE – determine if another position inside the organization would be a better fit; effect a transition

TERMINATE – if the performance does not get to the Target Performance Level for whatever reason, terminate the employee with dignity and mutual respect

Termination

- Prepare a script with HR including who will say/do what
- Anticipate potential reactions
  - Denial or shock – be clear, possibly refer to earlier conversations and warnings; allow time and silence as needed to sink in
  - Crying – allow time and silence; provide water or tissues; allow for space by leaving the room for a bit
  - Anger – ensure safe space and at least presence of one other person; possibly alert Security

RUMINATE – starting well before an employee is hired and continuing throughout and beyond, consider your actions and learning from your ongoing experience

Made in the USA
Lexington, KY
04 July 2015